A Primary Teacher's Handbook Reading

Frances Mackay

Acknowledgements

With thanks to the following schools:
St Mary's Primary School, Timsbury, Bynes
Colerne Primary School, Colerne, Wilts.
With thanks also to:
Jenny Elvin and the children in Year 6 at St Marys Primary School, Timsbury.
Photographs:
Bill Osborn

Material from the National Curriculum is Crown copyright and is reproduced by permission of the controller of HMSO.
Editor: Alison Millar   Design: Andy Bailey   Layout artist: Patricia Hollingsworth
Cover image: Bill Osborn   Cover design: Andy Bailey/Alison Colver

© 1996 Folens Limited, on behalf of the author.
Every effort has been made to contact copyright holders of material used in this book. If any have been overlooked, we will be pleased to make any necessary arrangements.

First published 1996 by Folens Limited, Dunstable and Dublin.
Folens Limited, Albert House, Apex Business Centre, Boscombe Road, Dunstable, LU5 4RL, England.

ISBN 1 85276 929-7

Printed in Hong Kong through World Print.

Contents

Introduction

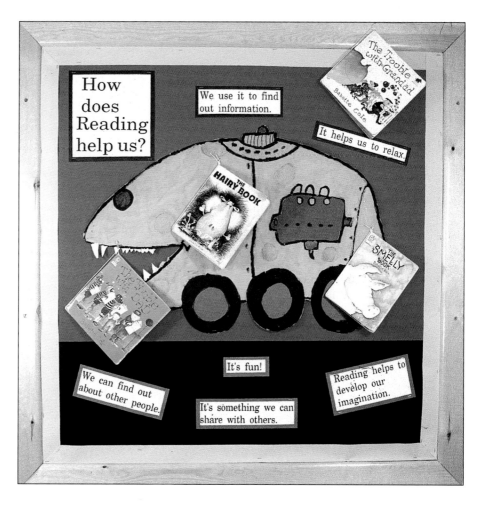

Reading has such a vital role to play in every child's learning that all teachers should gladly welcome supportive, practical guidance on the organisation, resourcing and assessment of reading.

This handbook aims to provide that support. It does not contain prescribed schemes or lessons but provides 'teacher-friendly' guidance concerning the requirements of the National Curriculum English document. It also provides guidance on activities that will enable progression through reading skills and reading experience. With guidance on writing a reading policy and scheme of work, suggestions for home reading, the use of computers, classroom management and assessment, *Teacher Handbook Reading* should prove an invaluable planning resource for every Primary class teacher.

Aims of the handbook

To support the teaching of reading by:
- ensuring good practice in reading education
- encouraging the children to experience a wide range of reading materials
- developing the children's ability to analyse and critically evaluate the materials that they read
- developing the children's creative and imaginative skills so that books can be shared, compared and emulated
- providing all children, regardless of ability, gender or race, with an opportunity to experience the enjoyment, stimulation and knowledge that books can provide
- encouraging the children's ability to articulate and communicate ideas, opinions and feeling about their own work and that of others
- providing the children with the experiences and skills necessary to enable them to become independent readers and learners.

Writing a policy statement and scheme of work

All schools need to produce a whole-school policy and scheme of work for reading.

The difficulty in carrying out this task often occurs because schools may be writing it for the first time with little previous documentation to work from. This books aims to help with this task.

The question thus arises: where do we begin?

Start with an audit
The points listed in the figure (right) will be helpful.

Where are we now?
Audit: existing policies, schemes of work, present reading curriculum, resources and time allocation.

Where do we want to be?
Eg: To have a clear and concise scheme of work that is regularly reviewed and flexible; to have a policy that allows for continuity, progression, breadth and balance.

How will we know when we have arrived?
Eg: Set a date by which you want the policy in place. Governors and parents will have been involved.

How do we get there?
Eg: By collaborating with staff; using support where available (eg advisory service and existing literature); by building on and extending resources by having a planned financial allocation.

English non-statutory guidance

What it says
A scheme of work is a written practical guide to teaching and describes the work planned for pupils in a class or a group over a specific period. It is an essential part of the school's responsibility. The scheme of work will include elements unique to English, and will show where English work supports, and is integrated with, other subjects.

Objectives
A scheme of work will detail the following:
- the content and sequence of lessons' progression and coherence and how they are assessed
- teaching methods and management of groupings
- how differentiation will be accomplished and provision made for individual children, including children with SEN
- provision for bilingual children
- the relationship between POS for English and those of other subjects
- methods of monitoring progress and achievement
- development of teaching materials and resources.

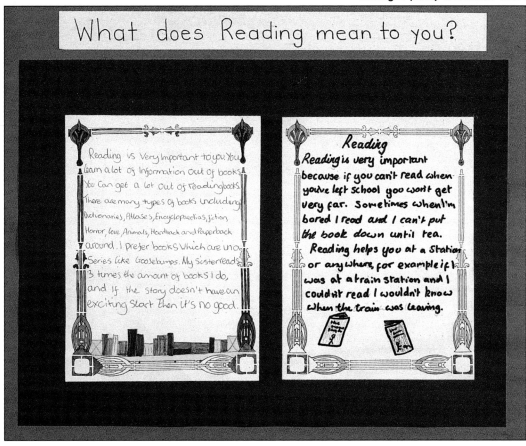

Elements of a reading policy and scheme of work

Three important questions need consideration:
- what do we teach?
- how do we teach?
- how do we know that children are learning?

The following headings may be appropriate when developing documentation:

Philosophy/Aims
What the school wishes to achieve, taking into account multicultural issues, equal opportunities and the children's enthusiasm and enjoyment.

Objectives
How the school will achieve its aims in relation to the National Curriculum.

Content
The themes or topics to be covered. The context for ideas and processes in relation to the Programme of Study.

Teaching and learning styles
The management and groupings of children. The overall approaches to the teaching of reading, classroom organisation, time allocation, cross-curricular aspects.

Differentiation
How this will be addressed. Learning outcomes. Consideration of children with SEN. Opportunities for achievement.

Continuity and progression
Continuity with previous and subsequent schemes of work. How reading will develop throughout the school. Progression in knowledge, understanding and skills.

Resources
The materials available and how they will be used. How outside agencies may be used. Financial allocation. Materials required.

Equal opportunities
How this will be addressed.

Assessment
Strategies to be used. Records and evidence to be kept. How to act on the information gathered. Sharing judgements and moderation.

Review
How and when.
What procedures will be used.

An example of a reading policy

Rationale

- It is through the teaching of English that all learning takes place. Competence in reading provides the key to independent learning and therefore the teaching of reading should be given the highest priority in our classrooms.

Purpose

- We teach reading for the following purposes:
  - to provide motivation and enjoyment
  - to develop the skills of independent reading
  - to develop reading as a facilitator for other curriculum areas
  - to enable the children to meet their reading needs as adults.

Guidelines

- Create a conducive reading environment with books that are stimulating, interesting, attractively displayed, wide-ranging and frequently updated with a wide variety of different presentations.
- Ensure the books are at a suitable level for the age, interest and reading ability of the children.
- Give reading a high priority by setting time aside each day for a quiet reading period.
- Foster a positive attitude to reading. Provide a good example to the children by sharing an enthusiasm for reading.
- Provide opportunities for the children to share books and reading experiences within their own class and across the age ranges.
- Develop critical appreciation by holding events such as Book Week and book fairs and invite people from the community.
- Provide opportunities for the children to partake in different kinds of reading experiences.
- Allow the children to browse through books and read 'lightweight' material for pleasure.
- Use the school library as well as class and other school book sources.
- Let children read aloud – to parents, to teachers, to other children, in group reading, using play readers, in assemblies.
- Provide a wide range of reading material – reading schemes, colour-coded 'real' books, reference books, newspapers and so on.
- Make use of listening centres and appropriate television and reading programmes.
- Teach appropriate reading strategies, including phonics, to help the children to read fluently, independently and with understanding.
- Encourage parents to read with and listen to their children on a daily basis.
- Use a reading booklet to record the home reading and to act as a means of home–school communication.

Assessment

- Standardised reading tests will take place twice yearly, in October and March.
- Teacher assessments will take place on a regular basis through reading conferences and observation.
- Standardised Assessment Tasks will take place at the end of Key Stages 1 and 2.
- A record will be kept of the children's progress and the titles of books read by each child.

Conclusion

- Our current aims are to improve the home–school reading liaison and to build up a better stock of reading material.

Review

- This policy reflects the consensus of the whole teaching staff and the governing body.
- The policy will be reviewed by the date indicated below:
  Review date:
  The implementation of this policy is the responsibility of all members of staff.

An example of a scheme of work for reading – Year 6

Lloyd and Greg have made a model village. Each building is a little book.

- The children will read from a variety of texts, including their own choice of 'real' books, group reading books, information books, books from the class library, school library and home, newspapers, magazines and reference books.

- Each child will read to the teacher at least twice a week – once during a group reading session and then individually. Reading groups are based on ability levels and the texts are selected to match these levels. The children can select their own reading book, under the teacher's guidance. There will be topic-based tasks during English lessons each day. Children with SEN will have a weekly action plan in which the teacher sets differentiated tasks. This work is reviewed every month. All children will have a Reading Together booklet in which the teacher and the parent write comments each time they hear the child read. Whenever possible, reading tasks will be related to the topic but more specific skills and experiences will be taught in ability groups as separate lessons. Bilingual children will have the support of the SEN co-ordinator and the LEA support staff if necessary, plus access to bilingual texts.

Reading programme

- Range: Reading from a variety of materials
  - Half an hour of silent reading on three days a week when the children select their own reading material.
  - Half an hour of shared reading two days a week from play readers, newspapers, magazines and reference books.
  - Once-a-week group reading where teacher and children share the same text.
  - Read to parents at least three times a week.
  - Use computer-based reading sources and word processing.
  - Use school library sessions to teach reference skills.

  - Read stories and informational writing to other children and to the teacher.

- Range: Information reading
  - information books
  - data-based computer programs
  - dictionaries, thesauruses and encyclopaedias
  - teacher-prepared activities.

- Range: Developing imagination and enthusiasm
  - Use interesting subject matter and settings which may relate to the children's own experiences or extend beyond the everyday.
  - Use books that benefit from being read aloud and re-read.
  - Use material with repetitive patterns.
  - Encourage more complex narratives.
  - Share books with a wide variety of organisational and presentational techniques. Discuss the illustrations used.
  - Make individual or class books.
  - Introduce stories and poems by significant children's authors.
  - Share traditional tales, classic poetry.
  - Use poems and stories set in a variety of situations – familiar, imaginary, fantasy, myths and legends.

Skills: Phonics and graphics

- By means of the above, the children will be taught to extend their phonic and graphic knowledge to include more complex patterns and irregularities and will include work on alliterations, sound patterns, syllables, initial and final blends, plurals, spelling patterns in verb endings, relationships between root words and derivatives, prefixes and suffixes.

Skills: Evaluation of text

- Comprehension activities that involve the use of inference and deduction.
- Whole class, group and individual discussions about the books they have read – plot, characters, ideas, vocabulary, illustrations, writing style etc.
- Use shared or group reading sessions to discuss the books read – using passages to illustrate and support ideas and opinions. Discuss why the children think the author included particular things, chose a particular writing style, used particular grammar and language.
- Use drama or puppetry to re-enact stories and poems the children have read.
- Provide opportunities for the children to share their ideas about the books they have read, particularly during school Book Week.
- Use the time when the child reads to the teacher to discuss in more detail the books being read. Have a weekly focus when listening to children read.

Skills: Finding information

- Use teacher-prepared activities, photocopiable material and books that provide opportunities for the children to distinguish between fact and opinion.
- Ask the children to write down questions they would like to find out the answers to – in all subject areas.
- Use class debates as a format for finding out information to support an issue. Give the children time to prepare and discuss an argument for the debate.
- Use dictionaries, thesauruses and glossaries to find out the meaning of unfamiliar vocabulary.
- Teach the children skimming and note-taking skills, using teacher-prepared and photocopiable material.
- Use computer programs, including CD-ROMS, to find out information.
- Use teacher-prepared and photocopiable materials for teaching summarising skills, finding the main idea of paragraphs, deciding which part of the material contains the information the children need.
- Discuss the meaning and use of newly-encountered words during individual and group reading sessions.
- Present information in a variety of formats – computer word processing, booklets, posters, leaflets, class English book, topic books and so on.

Topic-related activities and resources:
Britain since 1930

- Shared or group reading of relevant stories such as *I am David* and *Friend or Foe*.
  Use this time to discuss the content of the story as well as the way it is written – the language used, author ideas and bias, the children's own opinions.
- Reading stories and poems to the class from work produced in each decade.
- Use the computer program *Timetraveller* to find out information about Britain since the 1930s.
- Use library time for research.
- Use school log books to find out about life at your school over several decades.
- Use information books and other media.
- Use extracts from books to illustrate how the English language has changed since the 1930s.
- Discuss the text and illustrations used in story books from each decade – how they compare to today's books.
- Use teacher-prepared activities that involve the children in skills, such as summarising, finding the main idea, comprehension, author meaning and bias, fact and opinion and giving their own opinion about particular issues, articles and extracts relating to the topic.

Assessment

- The teacher will keep a reading diary of comments for each child. The diary will include comments about hearing the child read from reference books, the group reading book and the child's own reading book. Specific activities will be used to assess particular skills. In this topic these will be:
  - using an index page
  - finding information and answering a set of questions
  - distinguishing between fact and opinion
  - finding the main idea.

These targeted activities will be included in the child's profile and will be annotated. The child will also be asked to evaluate the topic him or herself in written or oral form. Things he or she will be asked to consider are: What new things have you learned from doing this topic? What did you enjoy most? What didn't you enjoy? Which books did you find most helpful to use? Why? What things do you find most difficult about doing research from information books? Are you pleased with your work for this topic? How do you think you might improve next time?

Reading in the National Curriculum

Key Stage

1

Roger Red-hat

Range

(1a) Provide a wide range of literature.
Children should read stories, poems, plays, picture books and their own writing:
– to themselves
– to others
– to the teacher.

(1b) Provide a wide range of information sources:
– IT-based
– dictionaries
– encyclopaedias
– fictional sources.

(1c) Develop imagination and enthusiasm:
– high interest
– clear ideas and themes
– clear expression and language
– pattern, rhyme and rhythm
– simple characters and plots
– wide variety of presentation
– stimulating illustrations.

(1d) Provide a wide variety of experiences:
– familiar settings
– imaginary worlds
– significant authors
– traditional tales
– range of cultures
– patterned language
– challenges in length and vocabulary.

Standard English and Language study

Provide opportunities to consider the characteristics and features of different kinds of texts such as beginnings and endings in stories.

Use reading to develop understanding of Standard English.

Key Skills

(2a) Pupils should be taught to read with:
– fluency
– accuracy
– understanding
– enjoyment.
Provide an extensive introduction to books, stories and words in print.
Teach the alphabet, sounds of spoken language, various approaches to word recognition and how to make sense of print.

(2b) Teach the following skills:
Phonics – sound patterns, rhyme, alliterations, syllables, initial and final sounds, blends, digraphs, patterns.
Graphics – plurals, spelling patterns in verb endings, prefixes, suffixes, root words and derivatives.
Word recognition – develop sight vocabulary, teach alternative meanings of words and phrases.
Grammar – teach how language is ordered and organised and how to use this to check meaning and accuracy.
Context – teach knowledge of book conventions, story structure, language patterns and presentation to help make sense of what is read.

(2c) Provide opportunities for children to:
– talk about characters, plots and language
– predict what might happen
– retell stories
– explain content
– choose their own books
– review their reading
– reread books
– listen to stories and poems
– act out the story of things they have read.

(2d) Teach how to use reference materials.

A PRIMARY TEACHER'S HANDBOOK – *Reading*

What the Programmes of Study mean

Range

(1a) Encourage pupils to develop as enthusiastic, independent and reflective readers.

Provide a wide range of literature.

Provide opportunities for children to read for pleasure.

Use progressively more challenging texts.

Allow children to read:
– on their own
– in pairs
– in groups.

(1b) Provide a wide range of information sources:
– IT-based
– newspapers
– encyclopaedias
– dictionaries
– thesauruses.

(1c) Include texts with:
– challenging subject matter
– more complex narratives
– more challenging ideas
– figurative language
– variety of structure and organisation.

(1d) Provide different categories of literature:
– modern fiction by significant authors
– long-established fiction
– quality modern poetry
– classic poetry
– variety of cultures and traditions
– myths, legends
– traditional tales.

Key Skills

(2a) To increase fluency, accuracy, understanding and enjoyment, teach more complex patterns and irregularities in phonics and graphics.

(2b) Provide opportunities for children to:
– respond to characters, plots, language, vocabulary and ideas in books
– use inference and deduction
– evaluate texts
– use texts to support opinions.

(2c) Teach how to find information in books and computer-based sources.

Provide opportunities for reading for different purposes.

Teach the following skills:
– skimming and scanning
– posing questions
– identifying what the children wish to know
– distinguishing between fact and opinion
– critically considering arguments
– using dictionaries, glossaries and thesauruses
– how to use new words
– how to re-present information.

(2d) Teach how to use library classification, catalogues and indexes.

Standard English and Language study

Provide opportunities to discuss different kinds of texts in terms of organisation, structure and presentation.

Encourage the use of reading to develop an understanding of the structure, vocabulary and grammar of Standard English.

Key Stage 2

Reading readiness

Children develop at different rates and vary widely in their abilities, skills and understanding. There can therefore be no decisive answers that can be given to determine when all children will be ready, but if teachers are sensitive to each child's differences and are aware of some of the factors that can contribute to readiness, then they can begin to observe and assess each child's stage of development.

Areas to consider are:
1 Physical – general health, eyes, ears, speech, motor co-ordination
2 Social/Behavioural – self-esteem, home experiences, social behaviour, cultural influences
3 Motivation – attitude, interest
4 Language – vocabulary, use of language, fluency, clarity, cultural consideration
5 Perceptual – visual discrimination, visual-motor co-ordination, visual memory, auditory discrimination, auditory memory.

CHECKLIST	SUGGESTED ACTIVITIES/RESPONSES
Physical – eyes Check school medical record. Check whether the child has been prescribed glasses. Check for obvious eye defects or injury. Observe any signs of visual discomfort – squinting, rubbing eyes, frowning, holding material too close or far away, red or swollen eyes, headaches, holding head in awkward position.	– Contact parents to discuss the problem. – Make sure the seating areas are well lit. – Seat the child near the board or work to be read. – Make enlarged drawings or texts if needed. – Obtain necessary advice from medical professionals.
Physical – ears Check school medical record. Ensure hearing aid (if worn) is on. Observe any signs of poor hearing . Failure to respond to questions or instructions, frequent requests for verbal repetition, inattentiveness, temporary hearing loss, for example colds.	– Contact parents to discuss the problem. – Seat the child near the source of sound. – Repeat instructions or explanations if necessary. – Use attention-getting devices – say child's name first, speak directly to child's face. – Provide listening activities such as taped stories where the volume can be adjusted.
Physical – speech Check school medical records. Listen for any differences in speech. Stammering, stuttering. Misuse of sounds – are some sounds substituted for others? Inability to make sounds.	– Contact parents to discuss the problem. – Make times available when the child can speak to you alone to avoid anxiety. – Don't hurry or complete the child's sentences. – Use auditory discrimination activities. – Seek professional help. Practise phonics.
Physical – motor co-ordination Observe any difficulties in control such as in painting, drawing, PE.	– Tracing activities. Finger plays, finger puppets. – Colouring activities, lacing, braiding, threading.

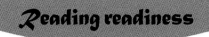

Reading readiness

CHECKLIST	SUGGESTED ACTIVITIES/RESPONSES
Social/Behavioural ☞ Observe any signs of anti-social behaviour – aggressiveness, inattentiveness, destructiveness, unresponsiveness. ☞ Is there a lack of home support?	– Seat child away from distractions. – Encourage child to read and reread favourite books. – Encourage paired reading to develop confidence. – Raise awareness of books – book discussions, making own books, sharing fiction and non-fiction, teach how to care for books. – Conduct regular parent evenings about reading. – Reward any positive behaviour.
Motivation ☞ Observe any signs of lack of interest in reading, reluctance, poor attitude	– Read a wide variety of books to the children. – Share your enthusiasm for books. – Encourage the children to make and share their own books. – Make interesting and inviting displays. – Promote books – book weeks, book fairs, library sessions, allowing children time to look at books. – Use a wide variety of responses to books – art, drama, puppets, music.
Language – speaking ☞ Is English a second language? ☞ How fluent and clear is the speech? ☞ How extensive is the vocabulary?	– Play games that encourage speaking. – Carry out group reading to discuss books. – Ask children to give a brief talk about an interest or hobby. Use a tape recorder if necessary. – Use big books to discuss text and illustrations with small groups or the whole class. – Share poems to discuss words and their meanings. – Provide bilingual books. Discuss other languages.
Language – listening ☞ Observe signs of inattention, not following instructions, not listening to others in group work.	– Seat the child away from distractions. – Read to the children often – discuss the book. – Play games that encourage listening – Simon Says, guessing taped sounds, whispered messages. – Use taped stories. – Praise the children for good listening. – Read stories and ask the children to clap whenever a particular word is read. – Use nursery rhymes, poems and alphabet books to discuss rhyming, letter sounds. – Foster skills that aid listening – lists, notes.

Reading rediness

CHECKLIST	SUGGESTED ACTIVITIES/RESPONSES
Perceptual – visual discrimination Can the child: ☞ recognise differences in colour, shape and size of objects? ☞ see external and internal differences in objects? ☞ reproduce 3-D shapes and visual patterns? ☞ distinguish between the main figure and the background? ☞ recognise pairs of words that are the same (initial, final letters, blends)?	– Use concrete objects – blocks, beads, pictures – as focal points for activities on size, shape, colour, space relationships, directions. – Use matching activities: shapes, pictures, words. – Play Snap card games. – Encourage discrimination between objects: largest, smallest, similarities, differences. – Complete pictures – drawing a whole picture from part of one. – Find the one that is different in a set. – Use mazes, patterns, dot-to-dot, find letters that are the same.
Perceptual – visual-motor co-ordination ☞ Does the child appear to be clumsy when picking up objects? ☞ Can he or she copy shapes, own name? ☞ Can he or she distinguish similarities and differences?	– Tracing activities, drawing between guidelines. – Identify similarities and differences, complete pictures to look the same. – Creative activities: cutting out, peg board patterns, printing, colouring within line, lacing.
Perceptual – visual memory Can the child: ☞ recall details of a picture? ☞ remember objects seen a short time ago? ☞ reproduce patterns and sequences after being viewed then removed?	– Play memory games: Kim's game, hold up flash card (child reproduces what was on the card), Snap games. – Make a sequence of beads on a string – ask the child to repeat it after looking at it for a few minutes. – Line up five children in order, disperse, ask a child to line them up in the same order. Increase the number of children in the line. – Sequencing activities: repeat the order of pictures or objects.
Perceptual – auditory discrimination ☞ Can the child identify common sounds? ☞ Can he or she identify differences and similarities between sounds? ☞ Can he or she keep in time in rhythmic activities? ☞ Can he or she say simple poems or rhymes? ☞ Does he or she mispronounce words? **Perceptual – auditory memory** ☞ Can the child carry a message? ☞ Does he or she understand concepts such as before, next, second?	– Listen to and record sounds heard. – Play games to discriminate between sounds. – Use tape recordings of sounds, listen to different musical instruments – discuss differences. – Sequencing activities: repeating rhythms. – Rhyming activities: making up poems, making rhyming books, matching pictures to sounds. – Play memory games: 'I went shopping and I bought', repeating clapping sequences. – Activities that ask the child to position himself or herself in time and space – use dance, PE.

A PRIMARY TEACHER'S HANDBOOK – *Reading*

Areas of experience

The headings are:

- **Range of literature**
  The types of reading experiences we should provide.

- **Information reading**
  The types of information material to which children should have access.

- **Developing imagination and enthusiasm**
  Information about the types of texts to be used to develop enthusiasm for books.

- **Categories of literature**
  The types of books to which children should have access.

For children to develop as effective readers, there are particular experiences that should be provided.

This section lists these experiences, together with suggestions for the types of activities that may take place in the classroom.

The areas of experience are presented in a progressive format from Reception to Year 6. This is to give an idea of the possible stages of development for each area, but it is important to remember that progression in any subject area is never strictly linear and that most children will demonstrate aspects of each stage, possibly within one activity or within one year group.

For example, when using reference materials, a reception child may be capable of using books listed as being suitable for older children. These guidelines aim to assist with the planning and organisation of suitable activities for a wide range of abilities.

For each area of experience, two activities are expanded on to give an example of how these areas might be developed.

Many of the suggested activities show the close link between reading and writing as it is through writing that children learn to read and it is through reading that children learn to write.

The areas of experience are based on the National Curriculum areas of Range and Key Skills, and are closely linked to the content of these sections. This book therefore will assist teachers in the interpretation of the National Curriculum document and in the planning of their reading programmes.

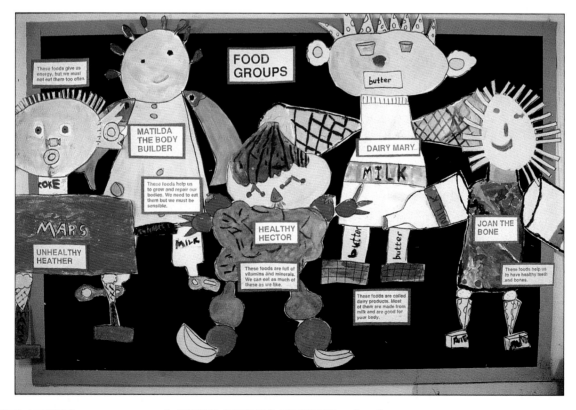

Progression through areas of experience

Picture books (fiction and non-fiction) with no or few words.

Alphabet books.
Nursery rhymes.

Labels/captions.

Range of literature

Nursery/Reception

Note: This progression is presented as a guide only. It is very important to remember that progression is not always linear and that any one child could be working on one or all of these stages at any one time.

Picture books (fiction and non-fiction) with words and sentences on each page. This may include reading scheme books.

Children's own writing.

Poems, rhymes, riddles.

Other children's writing.

Collections of short stories.

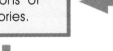

Longer texts with some illustrations.

Picture books with more challenging text.

Children's novels.

More challenging poetry.

Plays, eg *Take Part Series*, Ward Lock Educational.

Year 6

Information books with more challenging text.

A PRIMARY TEACHER'S HANDBOOK – *Reading*

Providing experience

Children should be encouraged to read on their own, with others, to parents and to teachers from a range of genres. Notice-boards and displays should actively invite attention. The wider range of media sources should also be made available.

EXPERIENCE	ACTIVITY SUGGESTIONS
Alphabet books/nursery rhymes	Teacher reads aloud. Shared reading. Making big books.
Picture books with no or few words	Tell the story and record it on a tape to go with the book.
Labels, captions	Make clear and well-presented labels. Write interesting captions.
Picture books with words and sentences	Fiction and non-fiction. Discuss cover and illustrations. Predict. Make and use a tape of the story. Retell the story.
Reading scheme books	Fiction and non-fiction. Use for group reading/book conferencing.
Children's own writing	Read their own writing aloud. Re-present it using IT.
Poems, rhymes, riddles	Favourite poem of the week. Make books and a card collection.
Other children's writing	Make hard cover books, big books, class books for the library.
Picture books with more challenging text	Paired reading, taking turns to read a page. Cut up old reading books – use pictures to make new books – children write the text.
Plays	Use play readers. Write and perform their own plays.
Information books with more challenging text	Use library times to discuss information books. Encourage children to write own information books. Read encyclopaedias, atlases etc.
More challenging poetry	Read out a poem a day. Invite a poet to visit the school.
Longer texts with some illustrations	Make a display of books by the same author – discuss/compare.
Collection of short stories	Write book reports about selected stories.
Children's novels	Multiple copies for group reading. Discuss fact/opinion, bias.

Other children's writing

Providing children with the opportunity of making their own books can be a valuable experience. These can take the form of whole class or group books where each child contributes one page. By making the books large, the teacher can then share the book with the whole class. The children can do paintings or drawings for each page and the teacher can act as scribe to write the words.

Older children can be shown how to make their own hard-cover books. The hard covers from old and damaged books can be removed to make new covers or the children can make covers from card.

Making shaped or pop-up books can prove a stimulus for writing. Look at published examples, such as *The Jolly Postman*, to motivate the children. Add their own books to the class library to elevate their importance and to promote self-esteem.

Children's novels

Group reading, where each child shares the reading of the same text, can provide opportunities for discussions about author style, plot, book organisation and presentation and use of language.

Other texts by the same author can then be compared with the first book to develop an awareness of author style and opinion. This could lead to a more in-depth study of one author where the children find out more about the author, carry out a class survey about the books written, write book reports about some of the books and note differences and similarities.

A multi-media presentation could be made about the author, using IT for word processing, tape recorders, photographs, paintings and actual books to provide the audience with a stimulating production.

18

Progression through areas of experience

Note: This progression is presented as a guide only. It is very important to remember that progression is not always linear and that any one child could be working on one or all of these stages at any one time.

Nursery/Reception

Television/video/radio.

Pictures/photographs. Simple information books with little text.

Simple information books with some text.

Teacher-prepared materials such as topic-related activity sheets.

Dictionaries.

Atlases/maps.

Posters/charts.

Information books with more detailed text.

Newspapers/magazines.

Tables/charts/diagrams/flow charts.

Thesauruses.

Encyclopaedias.

Other children's writing.

IT-based information programs/CD-ROM.

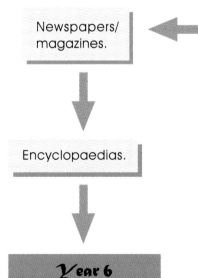

Year 6

A PRIMARY TEACHER'S HANDBOOK – *Reading*

Providing experience

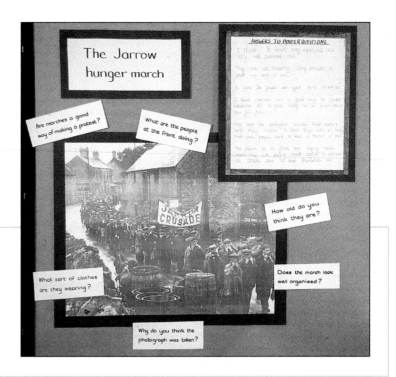

Children should have access to a wide range of sources of information to develop the skills necessary to become independent readers. They should be able to take home information books as well as story books.

EXPERIENCE	ACTIVITY SUGGESTIONS
Pictures/photographs and simple information books with little text	Discuss the pictures. Write the text for the pictures. Write labels, captions and sentences about the pictures.
Television, video, radio	Discuss the programme. List important points about it.
Simple information books with some text	Copy sentences from an information book and let the children draw pictures to match the text. Let them make their own.
Teacher-prepared material	Encourage the children to produce drawings, sentences, lists.
Dictionaries	Make activity cards. Play dictionary games. Make word cards.
Atlases, maps	Make atlas quiz sheets and maps of the school to help visitors.
Posters, charts	Write questions alongside posters and charts. Make into jigsaws.
Information books with more detailed text	Make an information book area in the classroom. Encourage children to bring in and talk about their favourite information book.
Other children's writing	Make information books. Use the computer for a final format.
IT-based information programs	Research specific topics. Use to make a book, poster or display.
Thesauruses	Find replacements for words in poems. Discuss the difference.
Tables, charts, diagrams, flow charts	Find the answers to a list of questions about the table or chart. Read a text and ask the children to draw a diagram of it. Compare.
Newspapers, magazines	Display interesting cuttings. Make a class newspaper or magazine.
Encyclopaedias	Compile quizzes from an encyclopaedia. Provide opportunities for reading encyclopaedias in silent reading times.

Using dictionaries

Play games to make the children more familiar with using dictionaries: races where they find particular words; a word of the day where they have to find out what it means and use the word in their work; make crossword puzzles using clues from particular pages in the dictionary.

Make class dictionaries of words pertinent to the class topic. Challenge the children to write some sentences using as many words as possible from a particular page in the dictionary.

Make word cards where the children have to match the card with the word and page of the dictionary.

Make up quizzes where the answers can be found in the dictionary. Have competitions on finding and using the longest or strangest word in the dictionary. Find unusual words – make posters of their meaning. Create a dictionary area with a variety of dictionaries, a poster telling children how to use them and paper and pencils handy for the children to use. Have an alphabet frieze nearby to help them to remember alphabetical order.

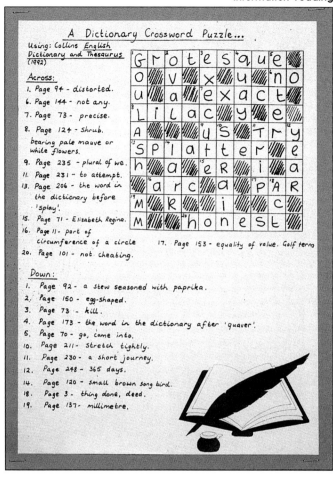

Using encyclopaedias

Make up some quizzes where the children find answers in the encyclopaedias, use index volumes to remind the children how to use them. Make posters on how to use the books. Use library times to practise using encyclopaedias – challenge the children to find out the answers to a few questions each week. Make a class set of encyclopaedias where the children each make a book of a particular letter of the alphabet – this could relate to the class topic.

Use CD-ROM encyclopaedias to find out the answers to a set of questions rather than about a particular topic – this prevents the children printing out huge quantities of information they do not need.

Make up question/activity sheets that relate to a particular page – use cloze procedure or ask the children to underline the main ideas (develops summarising skills).

Make a school encyclopaedia with details and facts for visitors.

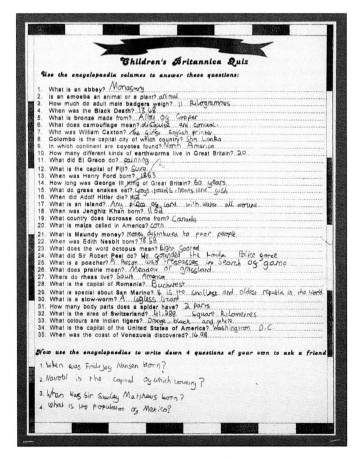

Progression through areas of experience

| *Developing imagination and enthusiasm* | *Nursery/Reception* |

Note: This progression is presented as a guide only. It is very important to remember that progression is not always linear and that any one child could be working on one or all of these stages at any one time.

Simple subject matter with high interest, exploring the pupil's own everyday experience as well as imaginary and fantasy worlds.

Books and poems with clear, simple ideas and themes, eg *Titch* by Pat Hutchins.

Texts with clear expression and language that benefit from being read aloud and then being reread, eg *Owl Babies* by Martin Waddell.

Texts with repetitive patterns, rhymes and rhythm.

Simple characterisation and plot, eg *Mrs Plug the Plumber* by Allan Ahlberg.

Wide variety of presentational and organisational techniques, eg pop-ups, lift-ups, such as *The Jolly Postman* by Allan Ahlberg.

Use of books with visually stimulating illustrations which enhance the text, eg *The Mousehole Cat* by Antonia Barber.

Progressively more challenging subject matter with broader perspectives, eg *A Taste of Freedom* by Julius Lester.

Progressively more challenging narratives and ideas, eg *I am David* by Ann Holme.

Poetry and prose that uses figurative language, eg *The Highwayman* by Alfred Noyes.

Year 6

A PRIMARY TEACHER'S HANDBOOK – *Reading*

Providing experience

Developing imagination and enthusiasm

Children should be exposed to the most exciting books available to stimulate their interest in the story, illustrations and overall book organisation and presentation. Teachers should enthuse about books and allow time to browse.

EXPERIENCE	ACTIVITY SUGGESTIONS
Simple subject matter with high interest	Display books on a theme. Add related pictures, models and objects. Read from the collection each day. Alternate the collection between everyday and fantasy topics.
Books and poems with clear, simple ideas and themes	Read a poem a day. Learn simple poems. Write out favourite poems as wall posters or big books – illustrate them. Make up simple group or class poems, add sound effects to them. Act out poems.
Texts with clear expression that benefit from being read aloud and reread	Reread and talk about favourite story books. Make big books using text from well-known books and children's own illustrations. Invite a favourite author to read to them. Have shared reading times.
Text with repetitive patterns, rhyme and rhythm	Read fairy tales, nursery rhymes, other rhymes. Make up different endings. Write alliterations. Make rhymes of children's names.
Simple characterisation and plot	Use picture books to discuss characters and plot – the main thing that happened, the main character. Change the ending.
Wide variety of presentational and organisational techniques	Look at pop-ups, lift-ups, black and white and colour illustrations, comic strips, no text and so on. Let the children make their own.
Visually stimulating illustrations	Discuss colours, texture, design, illustrations. Make wall friezes.
Progressively more challenging subject matter	Select books that will challenge children's thinking about the world around them. Use them to stimulate discussion. Hold debates.
Progressively more challenging narratives and ideas	Use extracts to discuss narrative styles when the children are writing their own stories. Let them copy a particular style or format.
Poetry and prose that uses figurative language	Read poems with figurative language. Select favourite lines or words. Find music to fit the poem's mood. Do paintings or drawings.

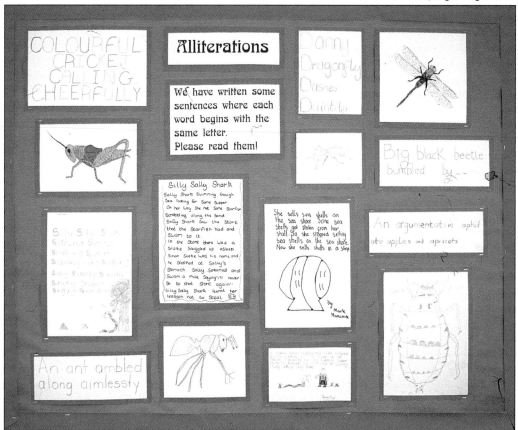

Repetitive patterns, rhyme and rhythm

Making up alliterations can be fun. For younger children, work with a small group to brain storm words of a particular letter. These could then be made into sentences with each word beginning with the same letter. With older or more able children use dictionaries and thesauruses.
These will provide an excellent source of ideas. The resulting sentences could be made into a book or a wall frieze.

Challenge the children to change the end words on lines of poems that rhyme. Discuss how this can change the whole meaning of the poem. Make riddle books and books of words that rhyme. Select a word for each letter of the alphabet and ask the children to think of as many words as they can that rhyme with them. Use the book to help with poetry writing.

Make up rhymes using the children's names.

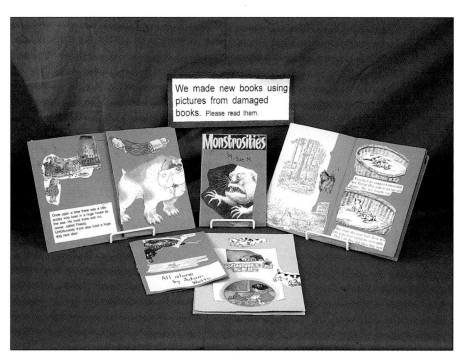

Using visually stimulating illustrations

Pictures cut out from old reading-scheme books or story books can stimulate ideas for new stories. If multiple copies of the same illustrations are available, the children's stories could be compared to discuss the alternative stories generated by the same pictures.

Cover the text in big books and ask the children to write some stories using the pictures. This will encourage them to look closely at what is happening in the pictures as well as looking at the sequencing of events.

Use large illustrations as starting points for story-telling.

Progression through areas of experience

Categories of literature

Nursery/Reception

Poems and stories with familiar, everyday settings.

Poems and stories about imaginary and fantasy worlds.

Traditional folk and fairy tales.

Literature containing patterned and predictable language.

Stories and poems from a range of cultures.

Myths and legends.

Wide range of modern and classic fiction by significant children's authors.

Wide range of good quality modern and classic poetry.

Literature taken from a variety of cultures and traditions.

Note: This progression is presented as a guide only. It is very important to remember that progression is not always linear and that any one child could be working on one or all of these stages at any one time.

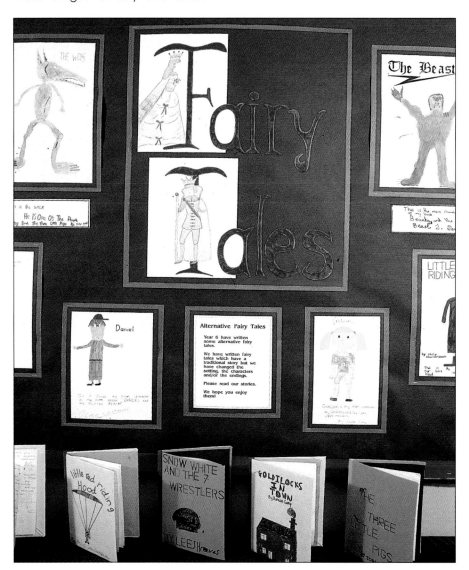

Progressively more challenging texts in terms of length and vocabulary.

Year 6

Providing experience

Categories of literature

It is important to offer children choice in their reading so that they experience a wide range of literary styles. They need to experience selecting and rejecting books and should be encouraged to select more challenging books.

Available texts should reflect the multicultural nature of society and include work by significant children's authors.

EXPERIENCE	ACTIVITY SUGGESTIONS
Poems and stories with familiar, everyday settings	Make 'copycat' versions, replacing names and places with the children's own. Make a big book about the school so that they become familiar with other teachers, classes and the school layout.
Poems and stories about imaginary and fantasy worlds	Discuss children's dreams and wishes. Make books about imaginary events. Read stories about mythical beasts. Make big books.
Traditional folk and fairy tales	Talk about how these books start and finish. Write tales using this pattern. Change the ending of a familiar story.
Literature containing patterned and predictable language	Use rhymes and riddles. Predict the last word of each line – how many different words would fit? Make riddle books. Copy out rhymes, leaving the last word blank for the children to complete.
Stories and poems from a range of cultures	Invite people from different cultures to read a story from their country. Discuss differences. Display books and artefacts. Have special weeks for different cultures with related stories and activities.
Myths and legends	Make up plays, puppet plays and dramas about the stories. Make up riddles where the children have to guess the mythical beast.
Wide range of modern and classic fiction	Display well-known, classic fiction and popular, modern-day authors. Read stories from each collection. Compare the differences and similarities about the stories and illustrations.
Wide range of good quality modern and classic poetry	Have a poem of the week, alternating between classic and modern. Invite poets in to share their poems. Make a book.
Literature from a variety of cultures and traditions	Share tales such as those from African, Indian and Aboriginal cultures. Compare text and illustrations. Use different styles.
Progressively more challenging texts	First, reading them as class stories. Reading the beginnings and encouraging children to complete them. Enthuse about books.

Categories of literature – stories and poems from a range of cultures

Begin a study of stories from other cultures by looking at collections of objects from that culture, such as religious items, artwork, fabrics, clothing and recipes. Can the children guess the culture? How different are the objects from other cultures? Read a story from the culture, especially if it contains references to some of the items on display. Discuss the meaning of the story. If possible, invite a person from this culture to tell or read a story. Make a group or class book using ideas from the story, collection of objects and the visitor. Use appropriate artwork for the cover pages and illustrations. Either the teacher or one member of the group could act as scribe for the group. Alternatively, each child could write a part of the story.

Make abc books, using words, art, designs, fabrics from different cultures.

Use picture books written in different languages. Can the children tell the story, using the illustrations as clues?

Modern and classic poetry

Make an abc book of classic poems, where each letter stands for a title, author, subject or first line. Ask the children to illustrate each page, using techniques and subject matter used in older versions of poetry books. Make another book of modern poetry, using modern art and design. Read a poem from the collections each day.

Make up class anthologies or poems on particular subjects or themes. Add this to the school or class library.

Make a poe-tree! Use a tree branch to hang leaves with favourite poems written on them. Change the leaves regularly, alternating between modern and classic poetry.

Make a permanent corridor display of favourite poems – each child and adult could write out or type and illustrate their favourite poem.

Organise poetry workshops for parents and/or children using local poets. Make a book of the poems written.

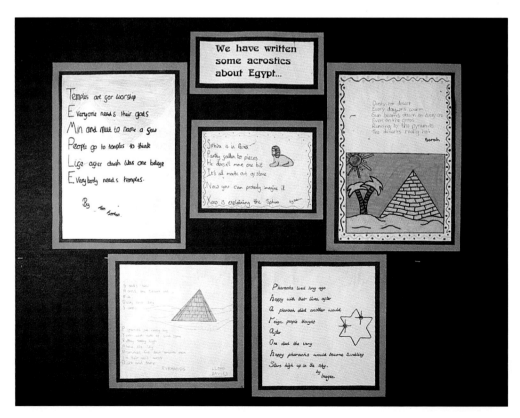

Areas of skill

Phonic knowledge
A suggested list of phonics that could be taught.

Graphic knowledge
The types of activities designed to develop understanding of words and their meanings.

Word recognition
Ways of developing word vocabulary.

Grammatical knowledge
Ideas for developing knowledge of syntax.

Contextual understanding
How to develop comprehension.

Responding to reading
Ways to encourage children to respond to reading in a variety of ways.

Using reference materials
The development of skills in using reference materials.

Standard English and language study
Some suggestions for the development of understanding of the use of the English language.

For children to develop as effective readers, there are particular skills to be taught that should be provided.

This section lists these skills, together with suggestions for the types of activities that may take place in the classroom.

The lists of skills are presented in a progressive format from Reception to Year 6. This is to give an idea of the possible stages of development for each area, but it is important to remember that progression in any subject area is never strictly linear and that most children will demonstrate aspects of each stage, possibly within one activity or within one year group. For example, when using reference materials, a Reception child may be capable of using skills listed as suitable for older children. These guidelines aim to assist with the planning and organisation of suitable activities for a wide range of abilities.

For each area of skill, two activities are expanded on to give an example of how these areas might be developed.

Many of the suggested activities show the close link between reading and writing. The two cannot really be separated, as it is through writing that children learn to read and it is through reading that children learn to write.

The areas of skill are based on the National Curriculum areas of Range and Key Skills, and are closely linked to the content of these sections. This book therefore will assist teachers in the interpretation of the National Curriculum document and in the planning of their reading programmes.

Progression through skills

Identifies initial then final sound in words.

Name and sound of letters of the alphabet.

Short vowel sounds.

Phonic knowledge

Nursery/Reception

Note: This progression is presented as a guide only. It is very important to remember that progression is not always linear and that any one child could be working on one or all of these stages at any one time.

Three letter words – consonant, vowel, consonant: cab, tab, bag, tag, map, sap, tap, mob, sob, mop, top, sud, fun, sun.

Syllabification.

Silent letters: b, c, g, h, k, l, n, p, t, u, ue.

Consonant digraphs: ch, ck, sh, th.

More complex patterns: age, alk, au, aught, dge, eight, ew, ey, ie, oe, oor, ough, ought, ould, ph, ui, ure.

Inconsistencies in phonic patterns, eg ea (heat) and ea (head), oo (book) and oo (moon), ow (cow) and ow (low).

Recognises alliteration, sound patterns and rhyme.

Prefixes: anti, con, dis, ex, im, in, ir, pre, pro, re, un.

Simple digraphs: ar, ai, all, aw, ay, ch, ck, ea, ee, er, ir, oa, oi, oo, or, ou, ow, oy, qu, sh, th, wh.

Two-letter initial consonant blends: bl, br, cl, cr, dr, fl, fr, gl, gr, pl, pr, sc, sl, sm, sn, sp, st, sw, tr, tw.

Suffixes and endings: able, al, ally, ance, dge, ed, eer, ence, er, es, est, ever, ful, fully, hood, ible, ing, ion, ish, ist, ity, les, less, ly, ment, ness, or, ous, sion, some, tion, wards, way.

How some letters influence the sound of others, eg 'magic e'.

Two-letter final consonant blends: fl, ld, lk, lt, mp, nd, ng, nk, nt, py, ry, sk, st, ty.

Year 6

Three-letter initial consonant blends: scr, shr, spl, spr, squ, str, thr.

Developing skills

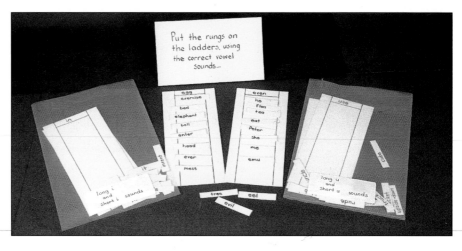

Phonic knowledge

It is important that children are made aware of the relationship between the letters of words and their sounds so that they are provided with one method of decoding and pronouncing words. They should know that many English words do not conform to phonetic rules. In developing phonic knowledge, children should be taught alliterations, sound patterns, rhyme, syllables, initial and final sounds, blends, digraphs and how some letters can influence the sound of others.

EXPERIENCE	ACTIVITY SUGGESTIONS
Name and sound of alphabet	Use: textured alphabets; matching games. Have a letter of the day.
Initial and final sounds	Match to pictures. Display word lists of initial and final sounds.
Short vowel sounds	Make a vowel sound ladder. Play Snap, matching the sounds.
Three-letter words	Find blends in books. Relate spelling and handwriting to blends.
Consonant digraphs	Make snakes and ladders games, using digraphs in each square.
Alliteration, sound patterns, rhyme	Write an alphabet alliteration, one letter/sentence per child.
Two-letter initial consonant blends	Use dictionaries to find words with the same initial blends.
Two-letter final consonant blends	Letter card games, eg Kim's Game; word bingo, blend riddles.
Three-letter initial consonant blends	Make up word hunts/crosswords using blends; word family lists.
Letters influencing the sound of others	Find words in stories with 'magic e'. Make sound mobiles.
Simple digraphs	Make up sentences: 'There was a mouse who lived in a house'.
Inconsistencies	List words with the same letters but different sounds.
Silent letters	Make wall charts of words with silent letters. Write 'kn' rhymes.
Syllabification	Haiku poems. Find little words in long words.
More complex digraphs	Sentences, eg 'The poor door was found on the floor'.
Prefixes	Write opposites, eg 'un' words. Discuss the meaning of prefixes.
Suffixes and endings	Relate to handwriting. Spelling rules for endings eg adding -ed -ing.

A PRIMARY TEACHER'S HANDBOOK – *Reading*

Phonic knowledge – consonant digraphs

Ask the children to use dictionaries to list all the words they can find beginning with or containing a particular digraph. Combine these to make a class list and add to it over time. Use the list to: write sentences using as many of the words as possible; write poems and rhymes; make a class book where each child writes sentences using the digraph and illustrates it; make cards to play matching/Snap games; use in handwriting activities; find the words in newspapers and magazines to practise skimming and scanning; make mobiles to use as word banks; write alliterations; make up puzzles about the list (My first is in ....., but not in ....); make story books where most of the words use the same digraph; make crossword puzzles; make family trees using a branch and leaves made of cards with the words written on them.

Syllabification

A good way to begin is to clap out the syllables in children's names, then go on to other words. Make jigsaws using simple compound words such as rain – bow, night – gown, or ask some children to draw pictures for the two words and ask others to guess what the whole word is.

Haiku poems are a good way to explore syllables. Read and discuss some first. Write out other poems on card and cut out each word – ask the children to make up the poem – how many different poems can be produced using the same words? Ask the children to write a haiku.

Play syllable card games – write parts of words such as in – stru – ment on cards. The children take it in turns to turn up two or three cards and try to make a word using the parts. A dictionary could be used to check answers.

Use percussion instruments to add interest to poems and rhymes – the children can play or clap on the syllables in the words.

Simple spelling patterns in verb endings – adding 'ed' and 'ing'.

Progression through skills

Simple plurals – adding 's'.

Simple compound words, eg into, rainbow.

Graphic knowledge

Nursery/Reception

Note: This progression is presented as a guide only. It is very important to remember that progression is not always linear and that any one child could be working on one or all of these stages at any one time.

Simple prefixes and suffixes, eg im-, in-, un-, -ed, -er, -est, -ful, -ing, -ly.

More complex plurals, eg adding -es to words ending in s, ss, sh, ch, x or z; changing y to i before adding -es; changing words that end in f and fe to v before adding -es; particular plurals such as child – children.

Diminutives, eg adding -ling, such as duckling; adding -et, such as locket; adding -ock, such as hillock; adding -icle, such as icicle; adding -ule, such as globule.

More complex spelling patterns in verb endings, eg doubling the last letter in words which end in a short vowel followed by a single consonant; dropping the silent 'e' before adding -ing; changing words that end in 'y' to 'i' before adding -es and -ed; changing words that end in 'ie' to 'y' before adding -ing.

Root words and derivatives, eg aqua – aquatic, liber – liberal, pro – pronoun.

More complex prefixes and suffixes, eg anti-, con-, dis-, ex-, ir-, pre-, pro-, re-, -able, -al, -ally, -ance, -ant, -dge, -eer, -ence, -ever, -fully, -hood, -ible, -ion, -ish, -ity, -less, -ment, -ness, -ous, -sion, -some, -tion, -wards, -way.

More complex compound words, eg heartache, knighthood, counterclockwise.

Year 6

A PRIMARY TEACHER'S HANDBOOK – *Reading*

Developing skills

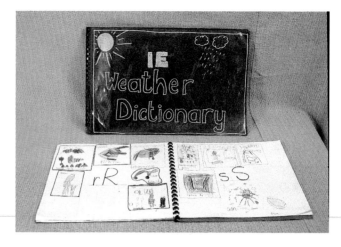

For children to understand more fully the meaning and usage of words, they need to explore letter patterns in plurals, verb endings, root words and derivatives, prefixes and suffixes. Drawing attention to these letter patterns will enable the children to use them more successfully in their own writing and to develop a greater understanding of the meaning of words in their reading.

EXPERIENCE	ACTIVITY SUGGESTIONS
Simple plurals	Look at plurals when reading big books. Make simple counting books: one cat, two cats. Match words to pictures.
Simple spelling patterns in verb endings	Make up simple sentences: I can jump, I jumped, I am jumping. Make them into books or a wall display. Make I, I am, I can cards and verb cards for making sentences. Discuss irregularities.
Simple compound words	Make jigsaw puzzles and Snap cards of compound words: rainbow. Display lists of compound words as word banks for writing.
Simple prefixes and suffixes	Use dictionaries to find words using the same prefix or suffix. Make a wall frieze of a particular prefix: 'in' words.
More complex plurals	Teach spelling rules and make mobiles for more complex plurals. Make a plurals mural which has different words: mouse, mice.
More complex verb endings	Teach more complex verb endings. Practise skimming to find examples in books. Make posters: fly, flies, flew, flying.
More complex compound words	Find small words in long words. Have a Word of the Week which is long and has many syllables. Centre activities around this word.
More complex prefixes and suffixes	Use dictionaries to find out the meaning and origin of more complex prefixes and suffixes. Discuss meanings of unknown words by drawing attention to the meanings of prefixes and suffixes.
Diminutives	Discuss how some affixes are commonly used to denote smallness: eaglet, owlet, leaflet, pamphlet. Find others and list them. Make crossword puzzles or word hunts of diminutives.
Root words and derivatives	Discuss how a meaning can change when a suffix is added: wonder, wonderful. Write sentences to show the meaning of the two words. Find out the meaning of root words: aqua, octo, pro. Find words that begin with these letters. Are the meanings similar?

Prefixes and suffixes

List prefixes or suffixes that have opposites in meaning: post- and pre- (after and before) or -ock and -oon (little and large). Ask the children to illustrate a word each and put these on display.

Have competitions to see who can find the most words with a particular prefix or suffix. Draw large ladders and write each word on a rung of the ladder. The class could make a ladder a week or each group could make their own ladder.

Make up crosswords or word searches using words of a particular prefix or suffix.

Make up story books using a particular prefix or suffix, such as The Important, Impudent Imp.

Make and display an abc of prefixes, showing the meaning of the prefix, examples of words with that prefix and sentences using the word. (Examples include: a, ante, bi, com, de, dis, ex, fore, grand, hydro, im, in, inter, kilo, mis, ob, post, pre, re, sub, trans, un, vice.)

Compound words

Combine compound words with words that rhyme and have the same number of syllables to make little rhyming sentences that can be illustrated, for example 'windmill, on the hill'; 'peppercorn, on the morn'; 'window-pane, will it rain?'.

Make a book of compound words with children's illustrations of each part of the word, such as 'underwater', with a drawing for under and one for water.

Use cloze procedure where the first or last part of a compound word has to be completed so that the sentence makes sense.

Write some beginning words of compound words on large dice (such as water, under, wind, black, high, key). The children roll the dice and say or write a compound word with that beginning. Dictionaries could be used to check the words.

Challenge the children to make word searches using compound words only.

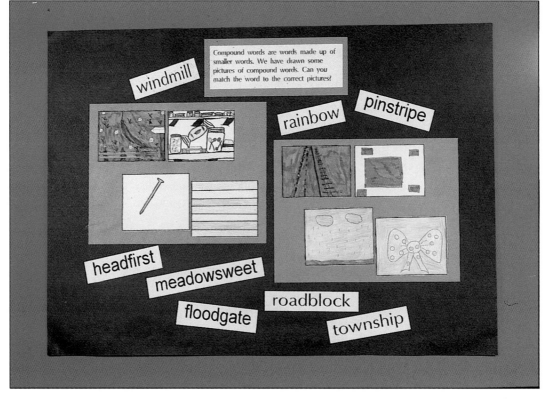

A PRIMARY TEACHER'S HANDBOOK – *Reading*

Progression through skills

Small word list of personal importance – child's name, I, like, my, mum, dad.

Word recognition

Nursery/Reception

Note: This progression is presented as a guide only. It is very important to remember that progression is not always linear and that any one child could be working on one or all of these stages at any one time.

Watch our word tree grow.

Small list of word groups, such as I can, I like, I am.

Key word list relating to reading scheme or reading book.

Sight vocabulary lists of most frequently-used words.

Lists of words with common letter strings and patterns.

Word lists of words the child wants to use in her writing.

Word lists which relate to the class topic.

Word lists of unusual or irregular words.

Synonyms, eg bucket and pail and antonyms, eg big and small.

Homographs, eg (carry) bear (animal), homonyms, eg novel (new), novel (book) and homophones, eg bear and bare.

Year 6

Developing skills

Word recognition

Encourage children to develop a vocabulary which they can recognise and understand automatically. At first, this will be a few words of personal importance but, as the reader develops, the list should focus on key words in the reading books used by the child and words with similar letter strings and patterns. Show them how to use this sight vocabulary to read unfamiliar words by referring to similar features, letter strings and patterns.

EXPERIENCE	ACTIVITY SUGGESTIONS
Word list of personal importance	Write words that are important to the child (own name) on card for reference. Play games with them. Use them in sentences.
Word groups, such as 'I can'	Make 'I am', 'I like' cards to be used to make sentences. Use the words as labels in the classroom: 'I can paint', next to artwork.
Key words relating to reading scheme or reading book	Write sentences using key words from reading schemes and display them with pictures from the scheme. Write the words on card and play games, such as Snap and alphabetical order.
Most frequently-used words	Make word jigsaws. Match the words to drawings of the word. Use cloze procedure where the words are missing from a sentence.
Common letter strings and patterns	Display the lists as word banks to use in handwriting and spelling activities. Make books about words with similar patterns: the 'and' book which has sentences with words that have 'and' in them.
Words the child wants to use	Give each child a page of boxes for each letter of the alphabet in which to write words he or she wants to use. Make card games.
Topic-related words	Make an abc book of words that relate to a topic. Make a wall mural of the topic, labelled with words and sentences about it.
Unusual or irregular words	Use dictionaries. Have a 'Strange Word of the Week'. Play odd one out – which word does not belong in the list?
Homographs, homonyms, homophones	Find the right word to make the sentence correct. Write poems using words of the same sound but different meaning. Display word meanings of commonly-confused words such as their/there.
Synonyms, antonyms	Build up a thesaurus of words that have the same meanings. Match opposites. Make up crosswords of synonyms or antonyms.

Common letter strings

A fun activity is to find words with 'ant' in them. List them and ask the children to take a word each and draw an ant looking like its meaning. For example, Santa, antique, elegant, pantomime, defiant, slant and pant. Other letter strings that could be used are: cat and dog.

To practise skimming, ask the children to race to find a word with a particular letter string in it from a page in a newspaper.

Read out or make up poems using as many words as possible with a certain letter string.

Make posters of words with commonly-used letter strings, such as -tion, -ing, -able, to put on display so that the children see them regularly and can refer to them while writing.

Make up sentences using words with the same letter string, for example 'The plucky duck drove the truck which got stuck in the muck on Mr Luck's duck farm.'

Topic-related words

Paint a tree with many branches and, as the topic progresses, add leaves with topic words. Some branches could hold words to do with particular aspects of the topic, for example a topic on water could have branches of fish words, river words and washing words.

Write topic words on cards, adding to them each week. Once a week the children could select an unseen card from the pile and find out its meaning. This would then be their word of the week. The children could use their word in sentences, draw a picture to show its meaning or they could be asked to explain its meaning to the class.

Make up crossword puzzles, word searches and cloze activities using the topic words.

Have a word box into which the children put words they do not understand. This can be useful if the teacher is working with another group or the child has limited dictionary skills. At the end of the week, the teacher could share the words with the children. The whole class could be asked to write sentences and draw pictures to show the meaning of words not previously understood.

Progression through skills

Using illustrations to 'read' a story.

Grammatical knowledge   Nursery/Reception

Note: This progression is presented as a guide only. It is very important to remember that progression is not always linear and that any one child could be working on one or all of these stages at any one time.

Recognising that text conveys meaning.

Using illustrations to assist reading of text.

Constructing and reading simple sentences.

Predicting possible words and phrases.

Sequencing – word order in sentences, story order.

Recognising features of text – alliterations, repetition, rhyme, rhythm.

Recognising links in text – conjunctions.

Constructing and reading more complex sentences – punctuation, verb tenses, adjectives, adverbs, nouns.

Year 6   ← Checking for meaning. ←

A PRIMARY TEACHER'S HANDBOOK – *Reading*

Developing skills

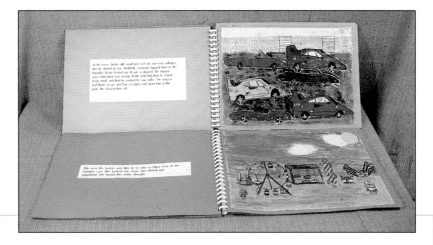

By developing a knowledge and understanding of the way language is ordered and organised into sentences, children are able to predict words, phrases and outcomes as well as developing strategies that enable them to check or confirm meanings in their reading. To achieve this, they should be taught to recognise the value of the surrounding text in identifying unknown words, to check the accuracy of their reading by listening to whether it sounds right, and to re-read or read ahead when the sense has been lost.

EXPERIENCE	ACTIVITY SUGGESTIONS
Using illustrations to 'read' a story	Make up a story about some pictures. Write the sentences underneath the pictures. Use pictures for sequencing activities.
Recognising that text conveys meaning	Using big books, point to the words as you read them. Relate them to the pictures. Ask the children to predict what might happen.
Using illustrations to assist reading of text	Show links between pictures and text. Ask the children to point to particular things in the pictures that are mentioned in the text.
Constructing and reading simple sentences	Make jigsaw-puzzle sentences. Make books using sentences where each child contributes a page. Cut up words of a sentence and ask the children to rearrange them to make sense.
Predicting possible words and phrases	Predict what the last word of a rhyme might be. Guess the end of stories with predictable and repeated patterns and phrases. Cover the text in a big book and ask the children to say what the story is.
Sequencing	Cut up and reorder stories. Discuss beginnings/endings – what words and phrases are used? Guess the middle of a sentence or story.
Recognising features of text	Use alliteration and rhyme in writing. Underline words that rhyme in stories or poems. Use cloze procedure to complete rhymes.
Recognising links in text	Write out parts of sentences on card, then conjunctions such as 'and', 'but', 'therefore'. Make sentences. Complete sentences using the same conjunction, such as 'because' or 'unless'.
Constructing and reading more complex sentences	Discuss punctuation, verb tenses etc. Compare the spoken and written word. Ask the children to check the grammar in their writing.
Checking for meaning	Reread or read ahead when meaning is lost. Does it make sense? Could it be improved? Rewrite jumbled sentences.

Sequencing

Type children's stories on to card and cut them up into jigsaw pieces. Ask the children to join the stories together so that they make sense.

Give the children a set of pictures and matching sentences. Ask them to match the picture with the correct sentence and then put all the sentences in order.

Use paragraphs from information books on the class topic – jumble the order and ask the children to sequence them correctly.

Have fun with spoonerisms where the first sounds of pairs of words are in the wrong order, for example 'fig on a palm' for 'pig on a farm'. The children can write the spoonerism and draw the answer so that others can guess its meaning.

Challenge them to unjumble the order of sentences that have a particular sequence, such as recipes or instructions.

More complex sentences

Use play scripts to practise reading aloud, using punctuation conventions such as commas and italics.

Type out a story or paragraph with incorrect punctuation and verb tenses and ask the children to edit it. Discuss the outcomes – does everyone agree?

Read a passage without pausing. Reread it, asking the children to tell you when they think a comma and full stop should be. Discuss why it may not make sense if a full stop was not there.

Tell the children about a conversation between two people. Ask them to write down the conversation, using correct punctuation and paragraphing. Discuss their work: have they included all the important details of the conversation? Talk about how to use the correct conventions, but also about how written language can vary from spoken language.

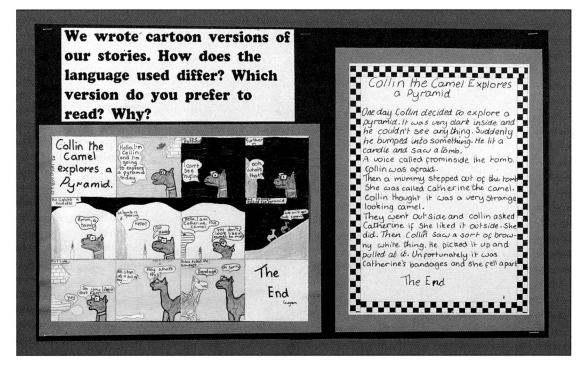

A PRIMARY TEACHER'S HANDBOOK – *Reading* © Folens (not copiable)

Progression through skills

Story conventions – beginning, middle and end.

Book conventions – title, author, page sequencing.

Contextual understanding and comprehension

Nursery/Reception

Note: This progression is presented as a guide only. It is very important to remember that progression is not always linear and that any one child could be working on one or all of these stages at any one time.

Retelling the story or facts – the main ideas, main characters.

Sequencing.

Making predictions, speculating, anticipating.

Cause and effect – identifying and discussing.

Making comparisons, discussing details, character traits.

What causes something to happen in a story? We looked at our favourite stories to find out.

Drawing conclusions.

Deriving meaning from figurative language – including colloquialisms, similes, metaphors.

Checking validity, author bias and opinion.

Year 6

Generalising, making judgements, detecting propaganda.

Developing skills

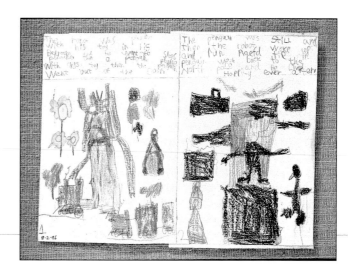

Deriving meaning from text is obviously the most crucial aspect of learning to read. At the literal level, children need encouragement to recognise the main ideas, the story sequence, character traits and story details, but perhaps the most difficult skills to teach are those concerned with the interpretation of the text or the 'reading between the lines' aspects. Children need a lot of practice to develop the skills of identifying cause and effect, drawing conclusions and making judgements. This is made easier by sharing and discussing the same text in a group.

EXPERIENCE	ACTIVITY SUGGESTIONS
Book conventions	Each time a book is read, draw attention to the title and author. Refer to the page numbers. Make books using these conventions.
Story conventions	Read from well-known stories – is it the beginning, middle or end? How can the children tell? Make books, allocating the sections to groups.
Retelling the story or facts	Use puppets or drama. Deliberately miss out an important part of a story – can the children tell what has been left out?
Sequencing	Rearrange a well-known story presented in the wrong sequence.
Making predictions, speculating, anticipating	Draw or write the missing part of a story. How might the story change if particular events/character traits were changed?
Cause and effect	Discuss a story: what led up to an event? What was the outcome of the event? What did the character learn from this event?
Making comparisons, discussing details, character traits	Discuss why the children think the author has used particular events and characters in the story. How does it compare with our own lives?
Drawing conclusions	Does the book have a message? Discuss fables and fairy tales.
Deriving meaning from figurative language	Look at the use of metaphors, similes, colloquialisms and onomatopoeia. Try using these writing styles.
Generalising, making judgements, detecting propaganda	Use extracts, from World War II for example, to discuss the use of propaganda. Read books where the character has to make a choice – is it the right one? Use comics to discuss generalising.
Checking validity, author bias and opinion	Write a biased piece about an event. Use it to discuss bias. Cut out different newspaper reports of the same event – compare them.

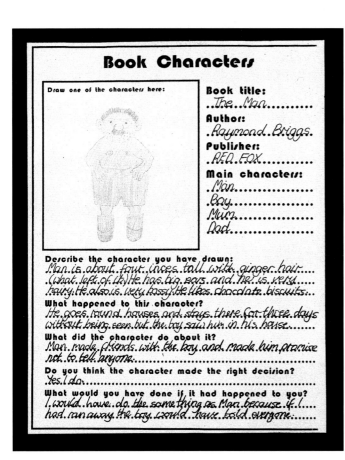

Making comparisons

Carry out occasional in-depth studies of characters in stories to provide an opportunity to relate character traits to our own behaviour, as well as determining how well the children have understood the story. This can include:

- writing out sentences about each character and comparing the responses
- finding specific words from the book that describe the character
- underlining words in book extracts that describe the character's behaviour
- discussing how the character's responses would compare with our own responses to the same situations
- discussing how the author has made us feel towards particular characters – are we meant to like or dislike them? What parts of the story support your view?
- discussing how characters in one story may compare with characters in another – do they remind you of other people in books and in real life?

Deriving meaning from figurative language

Discussions about colloquialisms can draw attention to the many words and phrases used in everyday language that have developed over time to mean something entirely different from the literal translation. Begin with a discussion about the meaning of terms such as 'a red-letter day', 'all ears', 'the man in the street', 'to draw the line', 'to smell a rat', 'a blind alley' and so on. List as many as you can. The children could draw the literal meaning and ask others to guess what the phrase is.

Use poetry to discuss the use of similes and metaphors. Ask the children to tell you why they think the poet has used such words and phrases.

How do they help the reader to understand what is happening?

Encourage the children to look out for similes and metaphors in the books they read. Build up a class list. Ask them to make up their own similes by updating some old ones, for example 'as quick as lightning' might become 'as quick as a computer chip'.

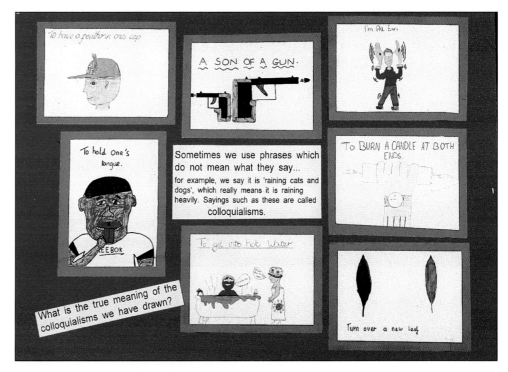

Progression through skills

Responding to reading

Nursery/Reception

Note: This progression is presented as a guide only. It is very important to remember that progression is not always linear and that any one child could be working on one or all of these stages at any one time.

Year 6

Listen to stories and information books being read aloud.

Talk about the books read – likes and dislikes.

Anticipate and predict what might happen next in a text.

Retell a story. Reread favourite books.

Choose books to read individually and with others.

Draw, paint, model or write in response to books read.

Review reading.

Explore content, plot, ideas and illustrations in more detail.

Discuss author techniques, book organisation and presentation.

Evaluate text – author opinion/bias. Give own opinions about texts.

Developing skills

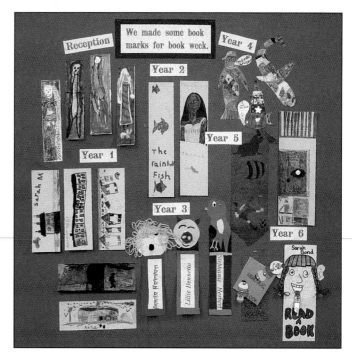

Responding to reading

👆 Children should be encouraged to respond to literature in a variety of ways. To explore a book thoroughly, they need to think about the plot, characters, setting, theme, style and genre. A variety of approaches ensures that all children's needs and interests can be catered for.

EXPERIENCE	ACTIVITY SUGGESTIONS
Listen to stories and information books being read aloud	Read aloud both new and familiar texts. Stop occasionally to talk about what has happened and predict what might happen next.
Talk about the books read – likes and dislikes	Discuss favourite books and characters. Talk about how stories begin and end. How are they different from information books?
Anticipate and predict what might happen next	Make up sequencing activities. Make up rhyming stories where predicting the next sentence is helped by using the rhymes.
Retell stories. Re-read favourite books	Ask the children to tell you their favourite story. Give them time to reread their favourite books. Discuss what they like about them.
Choose own books	Let the children select their own books, including non-fiction, to read individually or share in pairs. Display books by the same author.
Draw, paint, model or write in response to books read	Rewrite the story as a cartoon. Make posters to sell the book. Write a newspaper report about the main event. Turn it into a play.
Review reading	Hold book conferences and debates on choice of books and authors, information books, the best places and times for reading.
Explore content, plot, ideas and illustrations in more detail	Explore a passage or book in more detail. What is its main idea/event? How do the illustrations help you to understand it?
Discuss author techniques, book organisation and presentation	Look at pop-ups, folding books, different illustrative methods etc. Which types do the children prefer? Why are different techniques used? Let them make their own, using a variety of techniques.
Evaluate text – author opinion/bias. Give own opinions about texts.	Write about the story from the point of view of one of the characters. Does the story have a message? Find out about authors – does author life style/background influence the books?

Creative responses

There are many ways to respond creatively to reading. Here are a few examples:

- Make models of characters and settings from the book and display them together with writing about favourite parts of the story.
- Make hand or shadow puppets to dramatise the story.
- Rewrite favourite stories, changing the character or endings.
- Make a class newspaper with reports about characters from different stories.
- Write stories copying the author's style of writing.
- Write letters from one character to another from the same, or different, story.
- Dictate favourite extracts of books onto tape – let the children to listen to the tape in reading or library times.
- Write to authors or illustrators to question techniques, opinions and ideas.
- Use percussion instruments to make sounds/music to accompany the reading of a text.

Reviewing reading

Book reviews can become tedious if done too often or in the same format each time. Book conferences, which involve a more detailed discussion of the book a child is reading, could be done twice a term with the teacher. For other books, the children could be encouraged to keep a book review folder, containing the titles and authors of books read, together with a short comment about each. More detailed book reviews could be carried out termly or be planned to coincide with whole school events such as book weeks. Other ideas for book reviews:

- Prepare a talk to the class about a book or books.
- Plan a wall display about a book or author.
- Review one aspect of a book each week – characters one week, the plot the following week.
- Make book posters for the library.
- Hold debates about different aspects of books, such as black and white illustrations versus colour, or cartoon-style presentation compared with realistic representations.

A PRIMARY TEACHER'S HANDBOOK – *Reading*

Progression through skills

Familiarity with reference materials.

Nursery/Reception

Asking questions about a topic being investigated.

Recognising the difference between story and reference books.

Familiarity with content of reference books – headings, index, etc.

Using reference materials for different purposes.

Note: This progression is presented as a guide only. It is very important to remember that progression is not always linear and that any one child could be working on one or all of these stages at any one time.

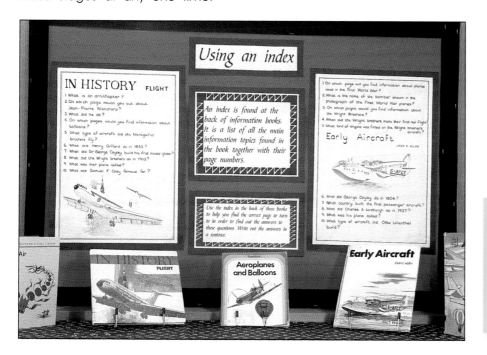

Finding information using:

pictures	contents
indexes	dictionaries
encyclopaedias	glossaries
maps	graphs
charts	tables
IT sources	thesauruses

Finding the main idea.

Distinguishing between fact and opinion, eg personal accounts of events written in history texts.

Representing information in different forms.

Recognising author bias, eg newspaper reports.

Using library classification systems, catalogues and indexes.

Year 6

Skimming, scanning.

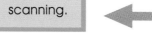

Making notes.

Developing skills

Using reference materials

Children should be taught to use reference materials for different purposes and how to find information in books and computer-based sources by using organisational devices to help them decide which part of the material to read closely. The development of such skills will enable them to become independent learners.

EXPERIENCE	ACTIVITY SUGGESTIONS
Familiarity with reference materials	Discuss content, pictures etc. Find books about specific subjects.
Asking questions	Discuss what to find out, how to find out. Using pictures.
Recognising reference books	Discuss the difference between fiction and non-fiction.
Familiarity with content of reference books	Find specific information using: contents, index, headings, captions, pictures. Compare the layout with story books.
Using reference materials for different purposes	Use IT-based sources to find and present information. Use headings only to locate information.
Finding information	Prepare questions that focus on different aspects, eg illustrations.
Finding the main idea	Underline the main idea/s. Draw a picture to represent it/them.
Representing information in different forms	Do flow charts or diagrams. Use computer presentations. Make a tape recording or video. Time lines. Drama, debates, plays.
Making notes	Write 5–10 facts from a passage. List important information.
Skimming, scanning	Look for key words. Use newspapers. Cloze procedure.
Using library classification systems, catalogues, indexes	Ask the children to sort the class library in some way. Discuss results. Make a catalogue of reference books for a class topic.
Distinguishing between fact and opinion	Use historical writing and newspapers to compare events. Use debates to provide opportunities to compare fact and opinion. Underline facts and opinions in passages.
Recognising author bias	Use advertisements to discuss bias. How can author bias affect historical reference materials? Compare different newspapers.

Finding the main idea

To help children find out the main ideas from a collection of texts, a useful activity is to divide them into pairs, naming one child A and the other B. Provide each pair with a text on the topic you are studying. Ask them to read the text and find out three things. Child A writes these down. After 5 minutes, ask child B from each pair to stand up and go to a different child A. The new pairs share what they found out (child B from the first text and child A from the current text). Change every 5 minutes. In this way, child A will write down a lot of facts and will know his text very well. Child B will have experience in meeting several texts and will need to remember some information in order to pass on this information to each new pair. After half an hour, discuss what the children found out as a whole class.

Ask the children to underline the main word or sentence from each paragraph of a text to find out the main ideas. Asking them to tell others what they found out is a good way of making sure they understand the information.

Skimming and scanning

Teach the children to find the books that are likely to contain the information they want by reading the title and the contents or chapter headings first. Then they can glance through to look at pictures, diagrams or maps. The index can then be used to locate the specific pages required. They can learn to read the first and last sentence of each paragraph on the page to gain an insight into the page's contents. Teachers can help by asking questions to which the answers will be found in each separate paragraph. The questions should have key words or phrases used in the text to help the skimming. There could be speed tests where the children try to improve their own time taken to answer a set of five questions. Ask them to underline the main idea of each paragraph. They can then use these sentences from each paragraph to write their own summary of the page or chapter.

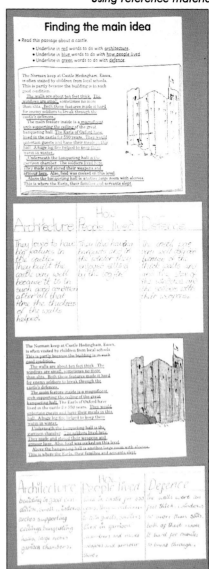

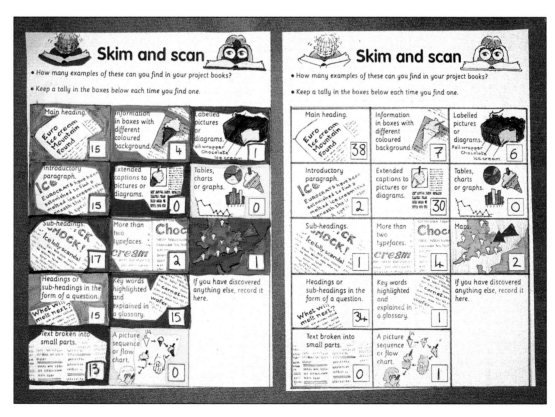

Standard English and language study

Standard English (SE) refers to the type of English that is usually used in print and is normally taught in schools. It is the type of English used in news broadcasts and other similar situations. Some children will learn SE because they are brought up speaking it, but others will develop a local dialect. It should be remembered that SE can be spoken with any accent. The teacher's role is to make the children aware of the structure, vocabulary and grammar of SE, without denigrating the importance of local dialect.

Language study involves the teaching of the organisational, structural and presentational features of different types of texts.

English non-statutory guidance

What it says

- Knowledge about language should be an integral part of work in English. Children learn what language is and what it can do through communicating with other people. As they become more knowledgeable about how language works, they become more sophisticated in its use. Their language development involves interplay between:
  – learning through language
  – learning to use language
  – learning about language.
- A central concern in work that explores knowledge about language should be the children's confidence and pleasure in language. An important way to develop children's knowledge about language is through reflection:
  – talking about how people use language
  – looking at how language is constructed
  – considering the effects of alternatives.
- Knowledge of linguistic terminology will help teachers to discuss pupils' language development. Terminology is taught to help pupils analyse their own use of language and, for example, the language used by novelists and poets.

Suggestions for activities

STUDY AREA	ACTIVITY
Beginnings in stories	Read aloud different story beginnings. Discuss the different styles/words used. Which do the children like best? Why? Look at fairy-tale beginnings – how similar are they? Guess the fairy-tale after hearing only the beginning.
Endings in stories	Discuss how fairy-tales usually end. Discuss alternative endings – do they always have to be happy? Ask the children to write their own endings for chosen stories.
Story dialogue	Use stories containing local dialects and accents to discuss the ways people speak and use language. Look at historical novels to compare the use of words.
Retelling stories	Use a tape recorder to record a favourite story. How is it different from a book? How can a speaker make the story interesting without the use of pictures?
Standard English	Watch a news report. How is it different from the way we might tell a friend about the same event? Let the children perform the report to practise diction and intonation.
Word study	Use poems to discuss the imaginative use of words. Explore onomatopoeia. Discuss why an author may have written in a particular way. Write poems with few words to stress the importance of using the 'right' word.

Home reading

Parents have a vital role to play in the development of their child's reading, so it is important for every school to establish good home–school liaison as part of the school's reading programme.

How can the school establish these links? Initially, it is essential that this is raised as part of a whole-school policy on reading, to ensure continuity throughout the school.

The school will then need to decide how best to approach the parents about, and how they will physically organise the process of, reading at home.

Many schools have designed a booklet that the children take home in which the teacher, the parent and/or child write the date, book title and relevant comments each time the child reads. These booklets can provide an invaluable means of daily communication between the parent and teacher and also serve as a reminder to the parents of the importance and value placed on reading by the school.

The school may also wish to organise a parent/teacher evening where the parents are invited to ask questions about learning to read as well as finding out how they can help their child at home.

The school will need to think carefully about the responses teachers make at such an evening, especially in regard to the advice they give to parents about helping their child when they make a mistake in their reading. If a booklet is produced, parental guidelines could form part of the information included in the introduction. It is also important that parents are made aware of the vital part they play as role models for their children. They should be encouraged to share reading with their children in lots of different ways – reading stories to them, shared reading of the same book, reading signs and notices and so on.

Ways to encourage good home–school links

- Use school newsletters to let parents know about good books to read, school book events and the school library loan system.
- Set up a toddler book-borrowing scheme at school to encourage parents to share books with very young children.
- Organise book swaps to save parents money. Invite the children to bring in good-quality books and comics they no longer need. Tokens can be given for each item donated. The children can then use the tokens to 'buy' a book from the collection.
- Organise book fairs or book weeks to raise awareness about books and authors.
- Encourage the children to take home non-fiction books sometimes to remind parents about the importance of reading a wide variety of books.
- Invite parents in to share a book with the class.
- Invite parents to use the school library themselves.

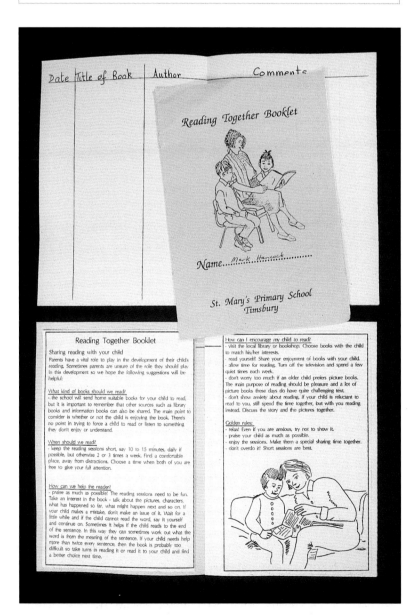

Computers and reading

Few teachers would doubt the valuable contribution Information Technology (IT) has to offer in the development of language skills. However, many primary schools only have one computer per classroom, so often the first concern to be faced by the teacher is how to successfully incorporate it into the daily literacy activities of the class.

Ideas for using one computer per class

- Make a timetable for individuals or pairs of children for half-hour computer sessions each week. This ensures that each child has weekly access where they can have more hands-on experience than when working in groups.
- Organise computer time as part of group working sessions so that each group has a computer session each week.
- Produce class books, magazines or newspapers, with each child contributing.
- Select software that can be used successfully by a group of children to encourage collaboration and a sharing of ideas.

How IT can specifically help reading

- Group word processing enables children to help each other with the reading involved, and promotes development of vocabulary.
- Simulations and database programs provide a sense of purpose for reading as well as providing immediate results.
- On-screen editing helps to eliminate frustration and time associated with editing by hand.
- A more attractive and authentic-looking end product encourages children to read the product and to feel proud of it.
- Many programs enable the teacher to tailor the reading to suit individual needs, thereby improving SEN access.

English non-statutory guidance

What it says

- English teachers have a responsibility for promoting Information Technology. It is important that teachers of English work with colleagues to develop policies for the use of IT.
- The decision to use a computer will enhance a particular programme of work being followed because a particular piece of software may allow children to use a particular kind of language or to reflect in a more structured way about a piece of text.
- IT can usefully help children to:
  - reflect on the demands of their readers
  - feel a sense of purpose in their writing
  - explore text leading to a greater absorption with its words and images
  - gain new insights into the text and its source.
- A computer database will help children to:
  - gather information and make it accessible to others
  - develop the skills of organising and presenting information
  - use the database to retrieve information
  - interpret and use the information.
- For pupils with special needs, IT may be an essential way of providing access to the curriculum.

Classroom practice and management

All teachers are keen to provide the very best experiences and learning situations for the children in their care, but the practical side of organising and managing a wide range of relevant and stimulating activities can be daunting. Where does the teacher begin? One starting point can be the physical arrangement of the classroom.

Class library or reading corner

The most obvious area to begin with is the class reading corner or library. The teacher needs to decide if he or she wants to have enough room in this area for the whole class to sit in comfort for story times and shared reading sessions, or if it is to be used mainly for group and individual activities. Whatever the main purpose, the area should be bright, attractive and stimulating. It should actively invite children to visit it and be a warm, cosy place in which to read books.

The books themselves should be displayed in an attractive way at a suitable height. Paperback books are best displayed on shelving that supports the books so that the front cover is facing outwards. The books should be organised into different sections, for example picture books, information books, poetry books, play readers, the children's own books, novels and so on. These sections should be labelled so that the children know where to return the books. Keep a box for damaged books so that they are identified and can be repaired.

Attractive book posters can be obtained from bookshops and library associations or the children can be encouraged to make their own. Active involvement in creating their reading environment will increase their enthusiasm for reading.

What it says

👋 **Key Stage 1** – Books should be properly displayed and accessible to small children. Selective use of captions, labels and explanations in the classroom should invite children to think, talk and respond, and relate purposefully to current work. In selecting books, teachers should note the quality of design and illustration, the interest of the narrative and the accessibility of the information. Teachers will decide how much support the child will need. They will ask the child to look back, or read on, in order to make sense of the text and will ask the child to make predictions and express an opinion. Children need to be encouraged to make choices from an early age in order to become independent readers.

👋 **Key Stage 2** – Children need to know how to find information. They need experience of browsing, selecting and rejecting books. They need to go beyond literal comprehension of the text. Production of their own writing will develop an awareness of the needs of readers. Teachers need to provide children with experiences that encourage closer reading and a variety of responses. They will need to provide activities which will lead the children to formulate their own questions, identify main points and gather relevant evidence from a number of sources.

Many teachers also provide cushions or easy chairs in this area to encourage a comfortable, relaxed attitude to reading. Most importantly, the area should contain stories the children have written themselves to promote self-esteem.

Management of the class reading corner

The selection of books for the class reading corner needs careful consideration. They should be of good quality with a variety of organisational and presentational techniques. The range of texts should be selected to cater for the wide range of reading abilities that usually exist within any one class and should include story, poetry, information and reference books.

The school might consider allocating a budget for class library books so that the books are replaced and updated annually. If funds are minimal, books can be obtained from other sources, such as:
– car boot sales
– donations from parents
– bulk borrowing from LEA or local library sources
– book fairs
– fund-raising events.

The management of the reading corner need not be restricted to the teacher. In fact, the involvement of the children themselves helps to create a more purposeful, successful resource. The children could be encouraged to:
– think up rules for using the library correctly
– help plan the reading corner itself
– help arrange monitors to keep the area tidy
– make suggestions for new titles
– generally be involved in the use of the area.

The teacher also needs to monitor the area constantly:
– Is it being used as intended?
– Is the area still attractive?
– Are the books being cared for by the children?
– Are the needs and interests of the children being catered for?
– What is/is not working well?

Ideas for creating a continued interest in the reading corner:
– Regularly change books that are shown front-on.
– Have an author or poem of the week displayed.
– Make regular displays of books by the same author or displays of information books on a particular theme.
– Regularly display the children's own writing about books.
– Add to the collection as much as possible.
– Replace tatty posters and books to keep the area looking attractive.

Management of other reading resources

There are many other resources apart from the class reading corner that need to be thought about. A separate reference area could be created where information books, atlases, dictionaries, thesauruses, magazines, newspapers, encyclopaedias and other reference sources are housed. This area could contain information on how to use encyclopaedias, how to use indexes and contents pages, how to summarise information, how to use dictionaries and atlases and so on. Like the reading corner, it should be arranged attractively and practically in order to create a purposeful resource in the classroom.

If reading schemes are used, thought should be given to access to and availability of the books and how the progression throughout the scheme will be organised and recorded. Careful consideration also needs to be given to the provision of experiences of 'real' books alongside the use of reading scheme material so that the children experience a wide variety of reading material.

If the school has a central library, how will this best be used? It is good practice to visit the library at least once a week and to use part of this time to practise skills such as using encyclopaedias, finding out information, using catalogue systems and so on. Consider how best to use the books available, including how the children borrow them and the usefulness of bulk borrowing for class use.

A PRIMARY TEACHER'S HANDBOOK – *Reading* © Folens (not copiable)

Planning for reading

Teachers have a challenging task when planning for the wide variety of experiences and skills essential to the development of reading. Perhaps the first consideration should be the school's Reading Policy and Scheme of Work because it is here that the teacher will obtain vital information about whole-school approaches and planning which will obviously have a direct impact on the teacher's own planning in the classroom. Reading records should provide a good starting point to build up knowledge about individual children's strengths, weaknesses and interests. Then can begin the planning of the experiences and skills the children should encounter during the year.

Planning considerations

The following should be considered when planning a suitable reading programme for the class:
– The abilities and interests of the children.
– Whole-school approaches to planning, organisation and record keeping.
– The physical organisation of the classroom resources.
– The approaches and methods to be used
– The range of materials available.

Many teachers adopt different approaches to the teaching of reading that allow for individual, group and whole-class teaching. How best to incorporate these methods into the daily teaching programme to maximise the benefit of each approach? The following things need consideration:
– How many times a week should the teacher hear each child read?
– How can the time best be used when hearing children read?
– How can the teacher assure quality time with each reader?
– How will the teacher record what happens when hearing children read?
– At what time of day is it best to hear children read?

– How useful is sustained silent reading (SSR)?
– Should the teacher listen to children reading during SSR or act as a role model and read herself?
– How long should SSR last each day? At what time of day should SSR take place?
– Will reading games be used? When? Who will use them?
– Will a listening centre be used? When? Who will use it? Where will it be located?
– What type of group activities will take place? When?
– What are the other children doing when the teacher is doing shared or group reading?
– When will whole-class activities take place? What kind of activities will benefit from whole-class teaching?
– Will book conferencing be used? When?
– How will the teacher communicate with the parents about their children's reading?
– What kinds of books will the children take home to read?
– How will the class and school libraries be used?
– How can the interests of the children be taken into account?
– How will the teacher ensure that the children have time to browse, select and reject books?
– What record will the children keep of their own reading?
– How can the teacher be kept up to date with new literature?
– What special provisions are necessary for children with special educational needs or bilingual children?

Perhaps the greatest problem is how to organise the week to meet all these needs. The following pages may provide some of the answers! The weekly planning of a Key Stage 1 and a Key Stage 2 class suggests some of the possibilities.

An example of weekly planning for reading – Year 2

TIME	MONDAY	TUESDAY	WEDNESDAY	THURSDAY	FRIDAY
8.45–9.00	Different table-top activities for when the children come in – jigsaw puzzles, left-right activities, sequencing, matching, handwriting.				
9.00–9.15	Book focus – looking at a collection of books which regularly changes. Could be author collection or subject focus – fiction and non-fiction. A different book is chosen each day to look at in more detail.				
9.15–10.15	Maths Journal work SEN children with GA support, work on key words	Maths	Group 1 – group reading using a big book Groups 2, 3 – using weekly plan to complete ongoing English work	Hall time TV – Words and Pictures programme	Groups 1, 3 – ongoing English work GA support for SEN Group 2 – group reading
10.15–10.30	Assembly				
10.45–12.00	Show and tell time Phonic activities – in ability groups Teacher hears 5 children read	Hall time	Maths	Class handwriting – linked to letter strings	Topic work – includes reading-related activities
12.00–12.20	Teacher hears SEN children read each day.				
1.15–1.30	Silent reading Teacher hears 5 children read	Reading partners Teacher hears 5 children read	Book reviews – oral	Silent reading Teacher hears 5 children read	Reading partners Teacher hears 5 children read
1.30–3.00	Planning time – children plan work in 3 areas Language work includes a reading game	Groups 1, 2 – using weekly plan to complete ongoing English work Group 3 – group reading using a big book Poetry – usually topic-based	Hall time RE work	Maths Class story	TV programme – related to topic

A PRIMARY TEACHER'S HANDBOOK – *Reading*

TIME	MONDAY	TUESDAY	WEDNESDAY	THURSDAY	FRIDAY
8.40–8.50 (before school)	Listen to one child read each day. This week's focus – to discuss the main character of the story, the traits, what has happened to the character, what the child thinks about the character and what she predicts might happen next.				
8.55–9.05 (during reg.)	All children practise spelling – look, say, cover, write, check. Group 3 have words with the same letter string.				
9.05–9.30	Group 1 – group reading / Reading with teacher, discussing story, author ideas, words used, responding to reading	Group 2 – group reading	Group 3 – group reading	Assembly	Assembly
9.30–10.00	Groups 1, 2 – writing a journal / Group 3 – with teacher / Discuss letter string or sound for the week. Revise the use of speech marks – look at examples in books. Play a game using letter string	Group 1 – with teacher / Discuss use of paragraphs. Activity – cut out paragraphs and put them in order to make sense. / Group 2 – topic related activity – using an index / Group 3 – follow-up Monday's work on letter string and speech marks	Group 1 – follow-up activity to Tuesday's work on using paragraphs / Group 2 – with teacher Introduction to use of paragraphs – looking at books to discuss / Group 3 – writing sentences or journal	Group 1 – writing a description using paragraphs / Group 2 – follow-up work on Wednesday's work on paragraphs / Group 3 – with teacher Revise week's work / Play a group game using letter string/sound	Whole-class activity – using topic-based reference books – using the index and contents pages
10.00–10.30	Groups 1, 2 – writing a magazine in pairs / Group 3 – writing a story	Group 1 – magazine work / Group 2 – handwriting linked to topic (teacher monitors group) / Group 3 – story writing	Group 1 – handwriting linked to topic (teacher monitors group) / Group 2 – magazine / Group 3 – story writing	Groups 1, 2 – topic-based research work / Group 3 – handwriting linked to letter string (teacher monitors)	Groups 1, 2 – choice of magazine or topic work / Group 3 – topic-based research work
10.50–12.00	Maths, geography activities. Things particular to reading include – using graphs, reading maths questions, using maps/tables. Class story will be read during this time for 10–15 minutes.				
1.15–1.45	Silent reading / Teacher listens to 5 children read	Silent or shared reading of topic books, newspapers or magazines. Teacher listens to 5 children read	School library visit – lesson on how to use index of encyclopaedias. Then free reading. Teacher listens to 3 children read	Silent reading / Teacher listens to 5 children read	Children read play reading books in groups, or do shared reading / Teacher listens to 5 children read
1.45–2.45	Group work and PE, music. Group work is topic-related and has these things related to reading – summarising information, using maps/tables, using computer-based information retrieval, using reference books, finding main ideas, using charts and posters, using television and radio programmes.				
2.45–3.15	PE – using work cards on sequencing and balancing		Music – writing own notation for sounds – playing and 'reading' the notations	TV programme – Carrie's War	TV programme – topic-related / Discuss

Assessment

Assessment lies at the heart of the Primary classroom because, by its very nature, teaching involves the observation of children, an assessment of their achievements and an evaluation and planning of the subsequent teaching and learning that takes place.

Types of assessment

- **Formative** – which finds out about the child's current achievements in order to identify his or her needs and ways of helping future progress (eg observations of the child reading).
- **Summative** – which provides an overall achievement (eg SATs results together with teacher assessments).
- **Diagnostic** – which identifies learning difficulties or particular strengths (eg miscue analysis).
- **Evaluative** – which uses aspects of school work as a means of assessing an LEA or part of the Educational Services (eg University research).

English non-statutory guidance

What it says

- The non-statutory guidance includes an opening quote from TGAT:
  'The assessment process should not determine what is to be taught and learned, it should be an integral part of the educational process, providing 'feedback' and 'feedforward'.'
- The guidance then goes on to say that teachers should adopt those methods of gathering evidence which best suit their own styles of teaching.
- It recommends that the non-linear development of children's language needs to be recognised and be provided for in any records kept.
- Records need to be based on more than one kind of recording, contain notes of performance over time and include information and observations from parents, other teachers and from children.
- It recommends that teachers should consider the factors that may affect their own judgements when observing and recording. These include:
  - the children's previous knowledge and experience
  - their linguistic experience and bilingual children's fluency in English
  - the organisation and presentation of an activity
  - the grouping of children
  - the ethos of the class
  - gender and cultural background
  - the special educational needs of particular children.

The purpose of assessment

- **To find a starting point for teaching**
  Effective teaching must begin with the child's current ability. Teachers need to know what a child can do in order to enable him or her to progress. Finding this starting point is one of the most important roles of assessment.
- **For feedback to the children**
  Informal praise or encouragement and written comments are ways of letting the children know whether they are meeting their own and their teacher's expectations.
- **For appraising and reporting individual progress**
  Records of assessments made on previous

occasions can be combined with current records to build a picture of change which indicates the extent of progress being made. Such information is important to the child's parents as well as the child's subsequent teacher.
- **For reviewing class and school performances**
  The publication of SATs results has been widely questioned and many schools refute the value of this kind of assessment.
- **For research**
  This enables monitoring of current practices and the development of new ideas.

Gathering evidence

Record keeping will vary from school to school, but it is important to develop a whole-school approach in order to achieve continuity within the subject areas. Any recording will need careful consideration so that the teacher's valuable time is not wasted in recording unnecessary information. Recording needs to be simple, relevant and not too time-consuming. The following questions may help when deciding on the types of records to keep:
Why record? Who is the record for? What will be recorded? When will the recording take place? How often? Where will the records be kept? How will they be organised? How much evidence will be kept? Who has access to the records? How will we ensure continuity and consistency in recording? What happens at the end of the year or Key Stage?

Ways of gathering evidence

- Teacher diary of observations/comments when listening to the child read.
- A list of the books the child has read, together with any relevant information.
- Formal reading tests – individual or whole class.
- Analysis of the child's reading (eg miscue analysis).
- Tape of the child reading.
- Child's own comments/reflections.
- Parent/teacher/child comments in home reading booklet.
- Child's reading journal.
- Written comments from parent/teacher meetings.
- Notes on child's reading interests.

Using the evidence

Perhaps the most important use of the evidence gathered is to help the teacher to plan the children's next stage of development. It should help to pinpoint weaknesses and strengths, their confidence and independence as readers and their reading tastes and preferences.

Evidence gathered over time is normally used to write a summary of the child's progress and presented in the form of an annual report to the parents. This report should be shared with the child to provide essential feedback and to help plan future work.

Miscue analysis

Almost invariably when reading a text aloud, children will make a response that is not in the text. Such responses are termed miscue rather than mistake because even good readers can include miscues and often it indicates a reader's strength, rather than a weakness. For example, sometimes a word is inserted on the basis of the child's accurate prediction of what the next word should be, thereby revealing a good understanding of the text as well as graphic and grammatical knowledge.

In general, the main miscues are:
– substitution – one word is substituted for another
– insertion – a word is added
– omission – a word is left out
– repetition – a word is repeated
– hesitation – the child pauses for a while
– self-correction – the initial attempt at the word is self-corrected

The information gathered from carrying out occasional miscue analysis will enable the teacher to determine the strengths and weaknesses of the reader in order to plan where to go next.

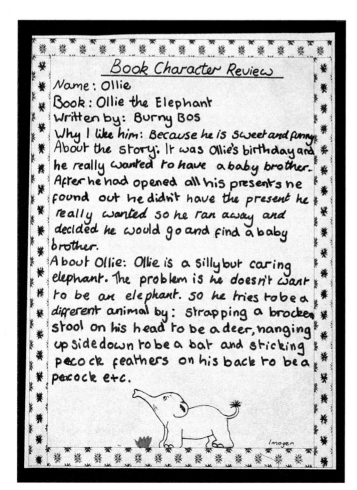

Miscue Analysis

Name. *Leanne M.*   Date. *13.3.96*

Text: Big Joe's Trailer Truck by Joe Mathieu.

This is Big Joe. He is a truck/driver. Joe arrives at the truck yard early in the morning. He waves hello to one of the other drivers in the yard.

First, Big Joe /reports to the dispatcher to get his orders for the day. He finds out what he is going to carry in his truck and where he is supposed to go. The /dispatcher gives Joe some maps and a time log.

Then Joe goes to the /service garage. His truck is being/repaired, and he wants to be sure it is ready.

The /service garage is a very busy place. Many mechanics work there, fixing any trucks that aren't running well. Sometimes they have to take a truck apart before they can fix it.

Joe's truck (is) ready to go. He thanks the/mechanics and drives out of the service garage. Joe drives across the yard to the terminal where all the trailers are being loaded. He backs up to the trailer he is to take out.

S = substitution   H = hesistation
I = insertion   SC = self-corrects
O = omission   W = word given
R = repetition

Book conferencing

Book conferencing involves an in-depth consideration of reading by the child and the teacher. The teacher should actively encourage the child to talk about his or her reading, not just the text at hand, but also in general terms to include interests and discussions about authors, favourite books and different writing styles. Teachers need to use questions that invite the child to talk more openly about the text being read.

Questions could include:
– Can you tell me why you chose the book?
– Have you read other books by this author?
– Can you tell me something about the main character?
– Does the author use special words or phrases that you particularly like? Can you show me an example in the book?
– What was the main event in the section you have just completed?
– Is there a problem to be solved in the story?
– Can you tell me about it?
– Tell me about the time when something important happened in the story.
– How do you think the people might sound?

Listening to children read

Perhaps the most difficult task for teachers is the organisation of listening to individual children read. No-one can doubt the benefit of one-to-one interaction but many teachers have real concerns about how to organise it and how best to use the time once it is planned. Perhaps the two main problems concerning listening to children read are: being distracted by other children or events in the classroom and how to listen to every child read every week without the process becoming boring or ritualised and therefore lacking any useful purpose.

Why listen to children read?

- To develop a love and enthusiasm for books.
- To find out the child's interests.
- To check on reading progress.
- To develop teacher/child relationships.
- To give the child practice in reading aloud.
- To share a common reading experience.
- To diagnose strengths and weaknesses.
- To develop fluency and accuracy.
- To share ideas about the book.
- To teach phonics in context.
- To develop comprehension and the use of contextual clues.
- To talk about author style, illustrations, book presentation, book characters and events.
- To develop intonation and expression.
- To discuss use of Standard English.

Ways to avoid interruptions!

- Use some non-contact time, such as just before school or the first ten minutes of lunch. Rotate the children so that everyone gets some of this time over a certain period.
- Make individual reading a 'bubble time' where no-one can interrupt you – have contingency plans – sets of games or activities they can use until you are available, a special signal to use in emergencies, and so on.
- Do not listen to readers during activities that need teacher monitoring.
- Wear a certain highly-visible item that signals no interruptions.
- Make sure other staff are aware that you do not want to be disturbed during this time – come to a whole-school agreement – perhaps common times of day for listening to children read.

Ways to ensure the time is 'quality' time

- Decide on a weekly focus that you will develop with each child, depending on his or her ability and experience. If this focus is planned on a half-termly or termly basis, it will help to ensure that the skills and experiences to be covered will be achieved. The focus could include: discussing the main character, looking at the usefulness and effectiveness of illustrations, discussing author ideas, bias and opinion, practising intonation and expression, finding out the meaning of newly encountered words, and finding the main idea of the page.
- Keep a log book of comments about the reading session. This will help in planning future activities and is a useful way to keep track of a child's interests, strengths and weaknesses. Keep recording to a minimum. Make this a useful, not onerous task.

- Make each session slightly different: share the reading sometimes to give the child a role model; begin in different ways – discussion, questions, looking at illustrations and so on. Make it an enjoyable experience for both of you!
- Let them pre-read the text they are going to share with you. This will give them more confidence and will also help to develop fluency. Sometimes the text could be read by the child and then just discussed with the teacher, not re-read. This will help to use the time wisely when the focus is comprehension.
- Sometimes use the session to do more detailed observations such as miscue analysis.
- Give older or more capable readers an opportunity to determine what happens in the session. Plan the next session together.

Reading resources

Reading Schemes

Foundations
Nursery to Lower Juniors
An innovative and exciting new reading scheme from Folens Publishers. It is the only reading scheme on the market that addresses the teaching of phonics in a creative and meaningful way. Divided into three bands – Emergent, Early and Experienced – it includes Big Books and over 200 fiction and non-fiction reading books across 17 levels of progression. The scheme also includes a comprehensive range of support material including a teacher manual for each band, 26 Letter Books with teacher notes, 30 Letter Cluster Books with teacher notes and copiable teacher resources for each band including homework exercises and activities that reinforce children's understanding of high frequency words and phonics. Additional resources include poster books, phonics CD–ROM, alphabet frieze and photograph flash cards.
Folens Publishers,
Albert House,
Apex Business Centre,
Boscombe Road,
Dunstable,
Bedfordshire LU5 4RL.
Tel: 01582 472788.

Collins Pathways
Reception to Year 6
Fiction and non-fiction books.
Good support materials.
Collins Educational,
Westerhill Road, Bishopbriggs,
Glasgow G64 1BR.
Tel: 0141 306 3455.

Story Chest
Reception to Year 6
Stories, poems, plays, information books and support materials.
Nelson, FREEPOST, ITPS Ltd, North Way, Andover, Hampshire SP10 5BR.
Tel: 01264 342992.

Wellington Square
Key Stage 2
Good high-interest, low-ability support materials.
Nelson (address as above).

Literacy Links
Reception to Year 6
Traditional tales, contemporary stories and non-fiction, poems, songs, teacher support materials and photocopiables.
Kingscourt Publishing,
PO Box 1427, FREEPOST,
London W6 9BR.
Tel: 0181 741 2533.

Phonics

Sounds OK and *Understanding Phonics*
Key Stages 1 and 2
Structured, photocopiable material with assessment.
Folens Publishers, Albert House, Apex Business Centre, Boscombe Road, Dunstable, Bedfordshire LU5 4RL.
Tel: 01582 472788.

Phonics Workshop,
Jackman and Frost
Cards, story-books, board games, cassettes, language master cards.
Blueprints – The Phonics Book,
Helen Hadley
Stanley Thornes,
Ellingborough House, Wellington Street, Cheltenham, Gloucestershire GL50 1YW.
Tel: 01242 577944 or
01242 228888.

Active Phonics
Graded workbooks.
Phonics Bank
Large discussion book, tapes and cards.
Ginn and Co Ltd,
Prebendal House, Parsons Fee, Aylesbury, Buckinghamshire HP20 2QY.
Tel: 01296 88411.

Fiction Sets

Literacy Centres
6–11 years
Good for group reading, teacher support book with activity ideas and photocopiables.
Scholastic Publications, Westfield Road, Southam, Leamington Spa, Warwickshire CV33 0JH, or Scholastic Publications, Clarendon Avenue, Leamington Spa, Warwickshire CV32 5PR.
Tel: 01926 887799.

Badger Reading Boxes
Reception to Year 6
Latest paperbacks graded for mixed ability use.
Badger Publishing Ltd,
26 Wedgwood Way,
Pin Green Industrial Estate, Stevenage,
Hertfordshire SG1 4QF.
Tel: 01438 356907.

Cambridge Poetry Box
6–12 years
Thematic poetry anthologies, three books for each level, good for group reading.
Cambridge University Press, The Edinburgh Building, Shaftesbury Road, Cambridge CB2 2RU.
Tel: 01223 312393.

Puffin Classroom Libraries
Years 1–6
Libraries for different age ranges, classics and new titles from a variety of cultures, teacher's notes.
Longman Group Ltd,
FREEPOST, Pinnacles,
Harlow, CM19 5AA.
Tel: 01279 623623.

Information Reading
Non-fiction Read-Abouts
Key Stage 2
Wide range of topical interests,
helps develop reference skills.
Kingscourt Publishing,
PO Box 1427,
FREEPOST,
London W6 9BR.
Tel: 0181 741 2533.

Learning Through Literacy
Key Stage 1
A box of books relating to a
topic, such as 'homes' and
'myself', lesson plans and
photocopiables.
Scholastic Publications,
Westfield Road, Southam,
Leamington Spa,
Warwickshire CV33 0JH,
or Scholastic Publications,
Clarendon Avenue,
Leamington Spa,
Warwickshire CV32 5PR.
Tel: 01926 887799.

*Ideas Bank – Information and
Library Skills*
5–11 years
Photocopiable activities to
develop reference skills.
Folens Publishers, Albert House,
Apex Business Centre,
Boscombe Road,
Dunstable,
Bedfordshire LU5 4RL.
Tel: 01582 472788.

Play readers
Take Part Series
5–10 years
Graded plays adapted from
well-known stories and tales.
Ward Lock Educational,
Ling Kee House,
1 Christopher Road,
East Grinstead,
West Sussex RH19 3BT.
Tel: 01342 318980.

New Reading 360 Plays
Reception to Year 6
Traditional tales and
contemporary stories.
Ginn and Co Ltd,
Prebendal House,
Parsons Fee, Aylesbury,
Buckinghamshire HP20 2QY.
Tel: 01296 88411.

Teacher Support Materials
Hooked on Books File
Helps teachers select fiction
from the wide range available,
gives a review, level of difficulty,
booklists for parents.
Collins Educational,
Westerhill Road, Bishopbriggs,
Glasgow G64 1BR.
Tel: 0141 306 3455.

Making Sense of Reading,
Nicholas Bielby
*Reading On – Developing
Reading at Key Stage 2*,
Dee Reid and Diana Bentley
(editors)
Scholastic Publications,
Westfield Road, Southam,
Leamington Spa,
Warwickshire CV33 0JH,
or Scholastic Publications,
Clarendon Avenue,
Leamington Spa,
Warwickshire CV32 5PR.
Tel: 01926 887799.

The Reading Handbook,
Bloom, Young, Waters
and Cotton
Reading Problems and Practices,
Jessie Reid
*Practical Ways to Teach
Reading*, Cliff Moon (editor)
Ward Lock Educational,
Ling Kee House,
1 Christopher Road,
East Grinstead,
West Sussex RH19 3BT.
Tel: 01342 318980.

The Phonic Reference File,
Gill Cotterell
Checklists, word lists and
diagnostic tests
Word for Word, Dee Reid
7–9 years
Ideas for SEN activities.
LDA, Duke Street, Wisbech,
Cambridgeshire PE13 2AE.
Tel: 01945 463441.

Learning to Teach Reading,
Geoffrey Roberts
Stanley Thornes,
Ellingborough House,
Wellington Street, Cheltenham,
Gloucestershire GL50 1YW.
Tel: 01242 577944
or 01242 228888.

On First Reading, James
and Kerr, and
Sounds Like This, Katie Kitching
Teacher ideas for early
reading skills.
Folens Publishers,
Albert House,
Apex Business Centre,
Boscombe Road,
Dunstable,
Bedfordshire LU5 4RL.
Tel: 01582 472788.

Assessment
Primary Reading Test
5–12 years
Word recognition and
sentence completion.
Suffolk Reading Scale
6–13 years
Comprehension, three levels.
*NFER-Nelson Group
Reading Tests*
6–14 years
Comprehension, screening
and SEN children.
NFER-Nelson,
Darville House,
2 Oxford Road East, Windsor,
Berkshire SL4 1DF.
Tel: 01753 858961.

WRaPS, Carver and Moseley
Key Stage 1
Word recognition and phonics.
Reading Progress Tests,
Vincent and Crumpler
Years 1–6
Edinburgh Reading Tests.
Hodder and Stoughton,
Hodder Headline Plc,
338 Euston Road,
London NW1 3BH.
Tel: 0171 873 6024.

Bankson Language Test,
Nicholas Bankson
Semantics and syntactics.
Taskmaster Ltd,
Morris Road,
Leicester LE2 6BR.
Tel: 0116 270 4286.

Glossary

Affix – a word or syllable added to a word to produce a derived form, a suffix or prefix.

Alliteration – the use of the same letter at the beginning of each word in a phrase.

Antonym – a word that means the opposite of another.

Auditory discrimination – the ability to detect differences and similarities in sounds.

Auditory memory – the ability to remember a sound.

Auditory perception – the recognition, discrimination and interpretation of sounds.

Book conferencing – an in-depth discussion of a book read by the child, not just at the literal level concerning characters and events, but at an interpretative level where the child is asked to consider his own and the author's opinions.

Cloze procedure – a technique used to assess comprehension where words are omitted and the child is asked to select an appropriate word to fill the space.

Colloquialisms – expressions commonly used in conversation, eg 'to nip in the bud'.

Compound word – a word formed from two or more existing words, eg, rainbow.

Conjunction – a word or group of words that connects words or phrases, eg, and, if, but.

Contextual understanding – deriving meaning from the text as a whole.

Digraphs – two letters, vowel or consonant, which combine to make one sound.

Diminutives – an affix added to a word to convey the meaning of small, eg, -let in booklet.

Genre – a kind or type of literary work.

Graphic knowledge – the development of an understanding of word meaning through the study of letter patterns.

Group reading – the sharing and reading of the same text by a group of children and the teacher.

Homograph – a word spelt the same as another, but having a different meaning.

Homonym – a word pronounced and spelt the same as another, but having a different meaning.

Homophone – a word pronounced the same as another, but having a different meaning or spelling or both.

Metaphor – a figure of speech where an implied comparison is made between two unlike objects or ideas, eg he is a tiger in battle.

Miscue analysis – an analysis of the types of miscues a reader makes when reading aloud. Such miscues include: substituting one word with another, adding a word to the text, leaving out a word, repeating a word, pausing for a long time and making self-corrections.

Onomatopoeia – a word which sounds like its meaning, eg hiss.

Paired reading – a beginning reader and an adult sharing a text chosen by the child or a more competent child sharing a book with a less able child.

Phonics – a study of the relationship between printed symbols and sound patterns.

Prefix – a letter or group of letters that precedes the word to which it is attached, eg un- unwell.

Propaganda – the promotion of certain information to assist or damage the cause of a government or movement.

Readiness – the level of development necessary to embark successfully on a new learning task.

Root word – a word in its first and simplest form, before affixes are added, eg plus – surplus.

Scanning – a reading technique to see if a particular point is present in a text or to locate it.

Shared reading – an adult and child sharing the same book with support, guidance and encouragement given by the adult. The two readers may take turns to read.

Simile – a figure of speech that likens one thing to another, usually introduced by the words as or like, eg as thick as thieves.

Skimming – a reading technique which involves rapid reading to decide what the text is about.

Standard English – the type of English usually used in print and normally used in news broadcasts and in schools.

Suffix – a letter or letters added to the end of a word to form another word, eg -ness in hardness.

Syllable – part of a word which is pronounced as a unit, eg person, per-son.

Synonym – a word that means the same as another.

Visual discrimination – the ability to detect differences and similarities in size, shape and colour.

Visual memory – the ability to recall a visual image.

Visual perception – the recognition, discrimination and interpretation of visual stimuli.